10
MINUTE
GUIDE TO
WordPerfect 6.1 for Windows

by Joe Kraynak

Revised by Jennifer Fulton

alpha
books

A Division of Macmillan Computer Publishing
A Prentice Hall Macmillan Company
201 West 103rd Street, Indianapolis, Indiana 46290 USA

MW00677978

To my kids, Nick and Ali, for making me laugh.—Joe Kraynak

To my sister Beth, one of my bestest friends.—Jennifer Fulton

©1994 by Alpha Books

International Standard Book Number: 1-56761-541-4
Library of Congress Catalog Card Number: 94-79167

96 95 94   8 7 6 5 4 3 2 1

Interpretation of the printing code: the rightmost number of the first series of numbers is the year of the book's printing; the rightmost number of the second series of numbers is the number of the book's printing. For example, a printing code of 94-1 shows that the first printing of the book was in 1994.

Screen reproductions in this book were created by means of the program Collage Plus from Inner Media, Inc., Hollis, NH.

Publisher: Marie Butler-Knight
Managing Editor: Elizabeth Keaffaber
Acquisitions Manager: Barry Pruett
Product Development Manager: Faithe Wempen
Production Editor: Kelly Oliver
Manuscript Editor: San Dee Phillips
Book Designer: Barbara Kordesh
Indexer: Rebecca Mayfield
Production: Dan Caparo, Brad Chinn, Kim Cofer, Lisa Daugherty, Cynthia Drouin, Jennifer Eberhardt, David Garrett, Erika Millen, Beth Rago, Bobbi Satterfield, Karen Walsh, Robert Wolf

Special thanks to C. Herbert Feltner for ensuring the technical accuracy of this book.

Printed in the United States of America

Contents

Introduction

Congratulations! You have one of the most powerful word processing programs on the market—WordPerfect 6.1 for Windows. With it, you can type and print a letter, memo, or report; check for errors in spelling and grammar; create your own newsletter (complete with fancy type and pieces of clip art); and do much, much more. That's the good news. The bad news is that you have to learn the basics before you can get anything done.

So, Now What?

You can wade through the manual that came with WordPerfect for Windows to find out how to perform a specific task, but that may take a while. Instead, why not use a more practical guide, one that tells you exactly how to create, edit, format, and print a document, without a lot of extra stuff you don't want to know or don't have time to learn?

Welcome to the 10 Minute Guide to WordPerfect 6.1 for Windows

Because most people don't have the luxury of sitting down uninterrupted for hours at a time to learn WordPerfect, this *10 Minute Guide* does not attempt to teach everything about the program. Instead, this book focuses on the most often-used features. We discuss each feature in a single, self-contained lesson, designed to take 10 minutes or less to complete. So whenever you have just 10 minutes, you can complete a lesson on how to edit, save, or even print a document.

This *10 Minute Guide* teaches you about WordPerfect without relying on technical jargon. The straightforward, easy-to-follow explanations and numbered lists tell you exactly which keys to press and which options to select. With the *10 Minute Guide to WordPerfect 6.1 for Windows*, learning to use the program is quick and easy.

Why You Need This Book

The *10 Minute Guide to WordPerfect 6.1 for Windows* is for anyone who:

- Needs to learn WordPerfect for Windows quickly.

- Feels overwhelmed or intimidated by the complexity of WordPerfect for Windows.

- Wants to find out quickly whether WordPerfect 6.1 for Windows meets his or her word processing needs.

- Wants a clear, concise guide to the most important features of WordPerfect 6.1 for Windows.

How This Book Is Organized

The *10 Minute Guide to WordPerfect 6.1 for Windows* consists of a series of lessons ranging from basics (such as starting the program) to a few more advanced features (such as working with graphics).

If this is your first encounter with WordPerfect 6.1 for Windows, work through Lessons 1 through 9 in order. These lessons lead you through the process of creating, editing, and saving your documents. Subsequent lessons tell you how to use the more advanced features to search and replace text, check for spelling and grammatical errors, change the style of the text, set the line spacing and margins, and print your document.

Icons and Conventions Used in This Book

The following icons have been added throughout the book to help you find your way around:

The text next to a **Timesaver Tip** icon offers shortcuts and hints for using the program efficiently.

Plain English icons are next to definitions of new terms.

Panic Button icons appear where new users often run into trouble.

You will find the following conventions that clarify the steps you must perform:

On-screen text	Any text that appears on-screen is in **bold**.
What you type	The information you type appears in bold and color.
Commands and Options	The names of menus, commands, buttons, and key combinations that you select appear in color.
Key+Key Combinations	In many cases, you must press a two-key key combination in order to enter a command, for example, "Press Ctrl+X." In such cases, hold down the first key while pressing the second key.

For Further Reference

To learn more about WordPerfect 6.1 for Windows, look for these books. They'll teach you how to use the program in a friendly, nontechnical way:

The Complete Idiot's Guide to WordPerfect for Windows, 2nd Edition, by Paul McFedries.

WordPerfect for Windows Cheat Sheet, by Shelley O'Hara.

Trademarks

All terms mentioned in this book that are known to be trademarks or service marks are listed below. In addition, terms suspected of being trademarks or service marks have been appropriately capitalized. Alpha Books cannot attest to the accuracy of this information. Use of a term in this book should not be regarded as affecting the validity of any trademark or service mark.

WordPerfect for Windows is a registered trademark of Novell Corporation.

Windows is a registered trademark of Microsoft Corporation.

Acknowledgments

Several authors wrote earlier versions of this book, and their great work made my job much easier; I am grateful. Thanks also to my wonderful teammates at Alpha Books, for their contributions to this work: Marie Butler-Knight, Faithe Wempen, Kelly Oliver, San Dee Phillips, Herb Feltner, and our great production team.

Lesson

Starting and Exiting WordPerfect for Windows

In this lesson, you'll learn how to start and end a typical WordPerfect for Windows work session and how to get online help.

Starting WordPerfect for Windows

Before you can use WordPerfect for Windows to type a document, you must start the program.

1. Type WIN at the DOS prompt and press Enter to start Microsoft Windows.

2. Double-click on the WPWin6.1 program group window to open it, if it's not already open.

3. Double-click on the WPWin6.1 program icon to start the program.

If this is the first time you've started the WordPerfect program, you'll see a message asking if you're interested in seeing a quick tutorial. If you click Yes, you will see a Welcome screen like the one shown in Figure 1.1. From here, you can start various coaches (interactive tutors) which introduce you to some of the basics of WordPerfect. If you click No, you'll be taken to an editing screen where you can begin typing.

Figure 1.1   Welcome to WordPerfect 6.1 for Windows!

4. If you'd like to view one of the coaches now, select one and then click on Continue. Otherwise, click on Skip this Coach.

5. Click OK.

> **I Want to Go Back!**   Never fear. If you skipped this coach because you were in a hurry today, you can still view it later. Just click on the Coaches button on the Toolbar and select the QuickStart coach. (You'll learn about the Toolbar in a minute.)

The WordPerfect document window appears, as shown in Figure 1.2.

Parts of the WordPerfect Screen

The WordPerfect document window (shown in Figure 1.2) consists of the following parts:

Title bar   Displays the title of the program you're running (WordPerfect) and the name of the document you're editing. If you haven't saved the document yet, a generic name appears (such as **Document1**).

Power Bar
Toolbar   Title bar   Menu bar

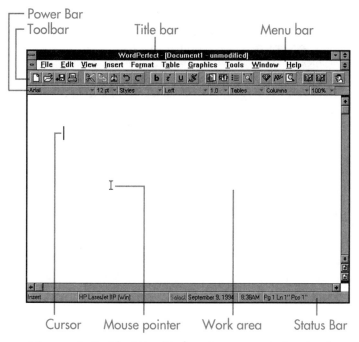

Cursor   Mouse pointer   Work area   Status Bar

Figure 1.2 The WordPerfect document window is where you start.

Menu bar Just below the title bar is the menu bar, which displays a list of menus you can open. Each menu contains a listing of related commands from which you can choose.

Toolbar If you've used a previous version of WordPerfect for Windows, you know this as the Button Bar. The Toolbar (its new name) contains buttons for quick access to common tasks, such as opening, saving, printing, and formatting your document. There are many toolbars from which you can choose; the 6.1 WordPerfect Toolbar (the default) is shown in Figure 1.2.

What's That For?   To see what a particular button does, rest the mouse pointer over it for a few seconds and then read the QuickTip. (The QuickTip is the yellow box that appears next to the mouse pointer.) While the mouse pointer is over a button, you can also look at the title bar for a description of the button's function. You'll learn more about the Toolbar and the Power Bar in the next lesson.

Power Bar   The Power Bar provides a series of buttons you can select to quickly perform common formatting tasks, such as changing the font, point size, or justification of text.

Cursor   The small, blinking vertical line in the upper-left corner of the screen is the cursor. Whatever you type appears at the cursor.

Work area   The main part of the screen is the work area. This is where you type your text.

Mouse pointer   If a mouse is installed on your computer, the mouse pointer appears on-screen. When it's in the work area, it appears as an I-beam. When it's over something that you can select or click on, like a button or scroll bar, it appears as an arrow.

Status Bar   The Status Bar at the bottom of the screen provides information about your document, such as the current date and time, and the location of the cursor. When you double-click on areas of the Status Bar, you access certain features quickly. For example, to insert the current date into the document, double-click on the Date area.

More Bells and Whistles   A Ruler Bar is also available, although it doesn't appear by default. The Ruler Bar is a ruler that you can use to change margins, set indents, and set tabs. You'll learn more about the Ruler Bar in the next lesson.

Getting Help

If at some point you're not sure what to do, help is only a few key strokes or mouse clicks away. Get help by performing these steps:

1. Open the Help menu.

2. Click on the help option you want:

Contents   Selecting this option allows you to go anywhere within the Help system. Browse through some examples or search for a particular topic. General help, such as information on using the keyboard, is also available.

Search for Help on   This option brings up a Search dialog box, in which you type the general topic for which you're searching. The available specific topics that match appear in a window for you to choose from (see Figure 1.3).

How Do I   The How Do I option takes a more practical view of help topics. It groups the help topics in logical categories, such as Create Documents or Format Document, and lists the most common topics under each category, such as My First Documents.

Type a topic to search for and
press Enter.

Select a topic from this list and
click on Go To.

Figure 1.3 Begin to type the topic you need help with, and a list of topics that match appears.

Macros The Macros option provides a list of help topics specifically for creating *macros*. Macros are recorded sets of steps for a task (such as the steps involved in printing a document) that you can use instead of manually selecting each step.

Coaches Coaches are online tutors that lead you through the process of performing a given task.

Quick Coach You can access the coaches quickly by clicking on the Coaches button on the Toolbar. Select a topic such as Headers and Footers, click OK, and you're on your way!

Upgrade Expert If you're moving to WordPerfect 6.1 for Windows from some other word processor (such as WordPerfect for DOS, Ami Pro, or Microsoft Word), you'll find specifics here for making the transition as easy as possible.

Tutorial   The Tutorial option lets you work through several lessons that teach you the WordPerfect basics. Repeat them as often as you like.

About WordPerfect   This option displays some general information about the WordPerfect program. If you entered your registration number the first time you ran WordPerfect, the information screen also displays that number.

Help When You Need It   To get help for a task you are currently trying to perform, start the task and work up to the point at which you need help. Press the F1 key, and Help comes to your rescue.

Exiting WordPerfect

When you finish working in WordPerfect, you can exit the program by performing the following steps:

1. Open the File menu and select Exit.

2. If you've made any changes to a document that you haven't saved, WordPerfect displays a dialog box asking if you want to save the file. At this point you don't, so press N to answer No. (If you do want to save, skip to Lesson 8 to learn how to save a file.)

Alternate Exit Routes   Here's another way to exit WordPerfect: double-click on the Control-menu box (the minus sign) at the very top-left corner of the WordPerfect for Windows screen. You can also press Alt+F4.

Lesson

2

Using WordPerfect's Tools

In this lesson, you'll learn how to use WordPerfect's Power Bar, Ruler Bar, and Toolbar, and how to control the on-screen display.

Using the Toolbar

Just under the menu bar, you'll find WordPerfect's Toolbar, which is shown in Figure 2.1. The Toolbar contains a series of small squares called *buttons*, which you can click on to quickly perform some common task, such as printing a document.

Toolbar   Menu bar

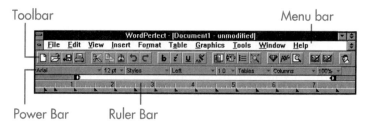

Power Bar   Ruler Bar

Figure 2.1   WordPerfect provides many tools to make your job easier.

There are many different toolbars from which you can choose, each customized to a specific task, such as editing, formatting, or working with tables. The 6.1 WordPerfect Toolbar (a generic toolbar containing buttons for general tasks) appears by default. Switch between various toolbars with help from the next section, "Switching to a Different Toolbar."

You can even move the Toolbar so it's located in a comfortable place on-screen, as explained in the section "Moving the Toolbar."

Out of My Way! If you'd like to get the Toolbar out of your way (remove it completely from the screen) so you can see more of your document, you can. Simply select View/Toolbar to toggle the Toolbar display on or off. To remove all the bars, select View/Hide Bars instead.

Look Who's Hiding! The 6.1 WordPerfect Toolbar contains more buttons than will fit across the top of the screen. To view the rest of them, move the Toolbar into the work area, as described later in this lesson.

The inside back cover of this book lists the buttons on the 6.1 WordPerfect Toolbar and their functions. You'll learn the specifics for many of these tasks in later lessons.

Switching to a Different Toolbar

WordPerfect comes with a variety of toolbars for various tasks. You can change toolbars by following these steps:

1. Move the mouse pointer between two of the buttons on the Toolbar.

2. Click with the right mouse button.

3. Select a toolbar from the QuickMenu.

QuickMenus   WordPerfect 6.1 for Windows offers fast access to common menu commands through the QuickMenu. Simply move the mouse pointer over the area you wish to work on, then click with the right mouse button. A QuickMenu appears with commands specific to the object to which you were pointing. Select a command from the QuickMenu by clicking on it.

Moving the Toolbar

You can relocate the Toolbar to any area of the screen:

* To place the Toolbar along an edge (such as the right-hand side of the screen), click on the Toolbar and drag it to the edge, then release the mouse button.

* To place the Toolbar within the work area, click on the Toolbar and drag it into the area. The Toolbar forms a resizeable rectangle.

* To resize the work area Toolbar, click on an edge and drag. When you release the mouse button, the buttons for the Toolbar rearrange to fit the new rectangle.

Using the Power Bar

Below the Toolbar is the Power Bar. The Power Bar provides you with a quick way to format your document, such as changing the font and size of text.

Monkey See, Monkey Do   Like the Toolbar, you can remove the Power Bar from the screen so you can see more of your document. Simply select View/Power Bar to toggle the Power Bar display on or off.

Table 2.1 lists the Power Bar buttons and their functions. To use the Power Bar, click on a button. Then select an item from the drop-down list, such as a font, a font size, or a zoom percentage.

Table 2.1 Here's what you'll find on the Power Bar.

Button	Function
Arial	Changes the font of selected text.
12 pt	Changes the size of selected text.
Styles	Changes the style of selected text.
Left	Changes the alignment (justification) of text.
1.0	Changes the line spacing of text.
Tables	Creates a table in the document.
Columns	Creates columns in the document.
100%	Zooms the text view in or out.

Using the Ruler Bar

The Ruler Bar is a tool that you can make appear at the top of your workspace. It displays the location of the left and right margins, indents, and tab markers for the current paragraph, as shown in Figure 2.2. Display it by selecting Ruler Bar from the View menu, or by pressing Alt+Shift+F3.

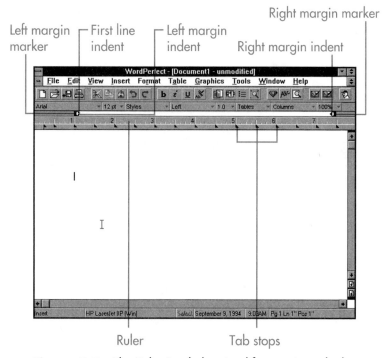

Figure 2.2 The Ruler Bar helps simplify margin and tab settings.

The Ruler Bar makes it easy to change margins, indents, and tab stops; just drag the markers to their new locations. To get rid of a tab stop, drag it *downward* off the Ruler Bar. You'll learn more about changing margins, indents, and tab stops in later lessons.

Changing the Screen View

In WordPerfect for Windows, text always appears as it will when printed, so you don't have to "preview" your document prior to printing. However, as you work, you have three choices for viewing the text on-screen:

- **Draft mode** displays the document without showing margins or the headers or footers. Page numbers do not display in this mode.

- **Page mode** shows the document as if the work area were a sheet of paper. If you have set a 1-inch top margin, for instance, the text appears 1-inch from the top of the work area.

- **Two Page mode** shows two pages of the document at the same time. Although text is more difficult to read in this mode, it's great for page layout changes, such as moving graphics and changing the columns in a newsletter.

To switch between modes, open the View menu and select Draft, Page, or Two Page. Page is the default setting; you can get back to it from either of the others by pressing Alt+F5.

In this lesson, you learned how to display and hide the Power Bar, Toolbar, and Ruler Bar, and how to use WordPerfect's three screen modes. In the next lesson, you'll learn how to start a new document.

Lesson

Creating a New Document

3

In this lesson, you'll learn how to create a new document—from scratch or with a template.

Starting a New Document

When you start WordPerfect for Windows, it opens with a blank page that's ready for you to begin typing. However, what should you do when you finish that document and you want another blank page so you can begin a new document?

With WordPerfect, you have two choices: you can begin a new document from scratch (on a blank page), or you can begin with a *template*. A template is like a form letter for a document; using one saves time in making your document look professional. You'll learn more about templates in the next section.

To start a new (blank) document:

1. Click on the New Blank Document button on the WordPerfect Toolbar.

> **Button, Button, Who's Got the Button?**
> If you're not sure which button is the New Blank Document button, simply move your mouse pointer over a likely candidate. A QuickTip appears, describing the button and its purpose. If you don't want to hunt around for the correct button, there's a guide to the Toolbar on the inside back cover of this book.

WordPerfect displays a blank page upon which you can enter text (you'll learn more about typing and editing text in the next lesson).

If you had an existing document open when you clicked on the New Blank Document button, it is still open—the new one is just on top of it. To move between open document windows, press Ctrl+F6 or select the document you want to move to from the Window menu.

> **Out of My Way!**   Before you begin a new document, you may want to close your old document first to get it out of your way. See Lesson 8 for instructions.

Starting a New Document with a Template

WordPerfect comes with many templates that you can use to begin a new document. A template is like a form letter for a particular document type, such as a letter, a memo, or a report. By using a template to create your document, you save time because the formatting (margins, line spacing, fonts, and so on) has already been placed in the document for you. Simply type in the text for the document and make moderate changes as necessary to fit your needs. For example, you can use a Letter template to create a professional-looking business letter in minutes.

> **Template**   Contains specifics for setting up a particular document type, such as a letter, report, or memo. A template can contain settings for margins, tabs, line spacing, page numbering, headings, and text attributes. In addition, a template can hold *boilerplate text* (reusable text, such as a closing to a standard letter).

Before we go on, I need to clear up some confusion about two of the Toolbar buttons. In the previous section, you were told to click on the New Blank Document button to create a blank document. In this section, you need to click on the New Document button, which sounds very similar, but which is actually a different button.

The New Blank Document button you used earlier is the first button on the Toolbar, and it looks like this: 🗋.

The New Document button that you'll be looking for in just a minute is located on the right, in the fourth set of buttons on the Toolbar, and it looks like this: 🖼.

Now that we've cleared that up, follow these steps to start a new document from a template:

1. Select File/New or click on the New Document button on the Toolbar. The New Document dialog box appears (See Figure 3.1).

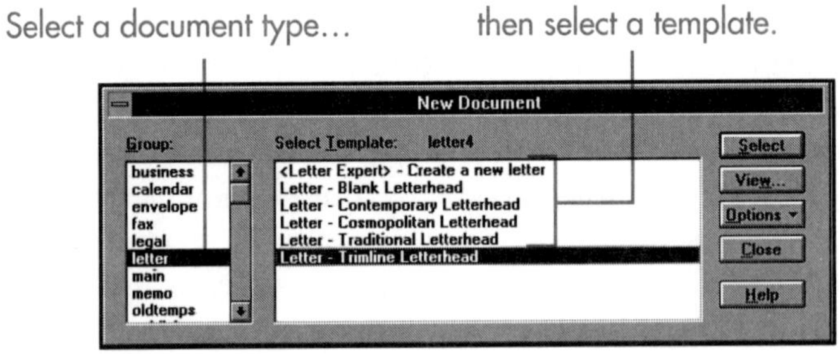

Select a document type...   then select a template.

Figure 3.1   The New Document dialog box.

2. Under Group, select a document type, such as letter or memo.

3. Choose a template from the Select Template list.

> **Ask the Expert**   If you'd like to have help in completing your document, choose an Expert instead. The Expert walks you through the process of selecting a template (or another file upon which to base your new document), entering text, spell checking, faxing, printing, and other associated tasks. Just select the Expert and follow the directions which appear. After

entering text, click on the Continue button in the QuickTask dialog box, and you'll be asked to select additional tasks you want to complete (spell checking, printing, etc.).

4. **(Optional)** If you want to look at a template before you open it, click on View. Another window opens to display the template. If you want to view another template, select it from the original dialog box. (Don't worry about this View window; it'll close by itself as soon as you select a template in step 5.)

5. Click on Select. A new document opens, based on the template you selected, as shown in Figure 3.2.

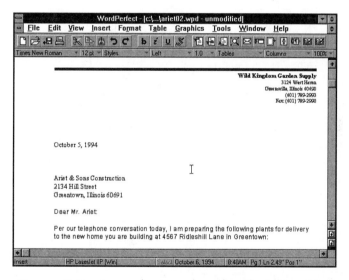

Figure 3.2   A new document based on the Letter - Trimline template.

Working with Templates

If this is your first time using a template, you'll see an Enter Your Personal Information dialog box (see Figure 3.3) asking you to enter some basic information, such as name and company. WordPerfect uses this information with the template to complete parts of your new document automatically. Type the needed information and click OK.

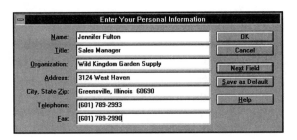

Figure 3.3   The Enter Your Personal Information dialog box.

Changing Times   If you need to change your personal information at a later date, look for a Template Fill button (or some such) on the Default Toolbar and make your changes.

You'll probably see an additional dialog box, asking you for information pertaining to the template itself, such as a recipient's name and address. You can add the addresses you use often to a permanent list by clicking on the Address Book button.

Each template comes with a customized toolbar with a full array of buttons that compliment the template type. For example, the letter templates come with a Closing button for creating a proper closing with notations for typist's initials, enclosures, and so on. If you choose a Letter template, there's even a button for inserting prewritten letter text, such as a welcome letter to a new employee. To find out what each button does, simply move the mouse pointer over the button and look for the QuickTip description that appears.

Lesson

Typing Text

In this lesson, you'll learn how to type text in a document and move the cursor around with the keyboard and mouse.

Entering Text

To enter text in WordPerfect, simply start typing. The characters you type appear on-screen at the *cursor* (the blinking vertical line). You can insert new text by moving the cursor to the point where you want to begin inserting (the insertion point), and then typing. You'll learn how to move the cursor around in the next section.

As you type, keep the following tips in mind:

- Press Enter only when you want to end a paragraph or a short line, such as a heading. WordPerfect automatically wraps text from the end of one line to the beginning of the next as you type. *Don't press Enter to move the cursor to the next line* within a paragraph as you would do with the carriage return on a typewriter (see Figure 4.1). Press Enter twice at the end of a paragraph to insert a blank line between that paragraph and the next.

- Press the Tab key at the beginning of a paragraph to indent the first line of a paragraph five spaces. You can create an automatic indent with the Indent feature (see Lesson 16), and skip the Tab key totally.

- You cannot use the down arrow key to move down until you have some text to move down to. Press Enter to move down, which essentially creates a new blank line.

- After you type a large amount of text, the text at the beginning of your document scrolls off the top of the screen. The text is still there; you just can't see it. You will learn how to bring this text into view (how to view a previous page of your document, for example) later in this lesson.

Press Enter to end a paragraph—
or to end a short line.

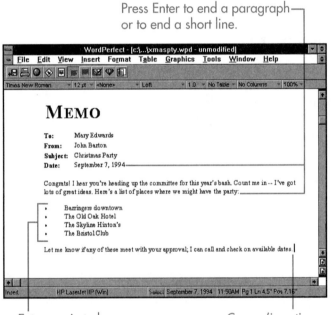

Press Enter again to leave a
blank line between paragraphs.

Cursor (insertion point)

Figure 4.1 As you type, WordPerfect wraps text from one line to the next.

Tiny Text Don't strain your eyes! If the text is hard to read, zoom in on it. Click on the Zoom button on the Power Bar (the one with the percentage in it, such as 100%), or open the View menu and select Zoom. Choose the desired zoom percentage from the list (150% works well).

Moving Around in a Document

Once you have some text on-screen, you can start moving the cursor (insertion point) around inside the document. You can move the cursor using either the keyboard or the mouse, as explained in the following sections.

Using Your Keyboard

Before you can start editing your document or formatting your text, you must know how to move around inside a document. To move around with the keyboard, use the keys listed in Table 4.1.

Table 4.1 Cursor-movement keys.

Press	To Move
↑	Up one line.
↓	Down one line.
←	One character to the left.
→	One character to the right.
Ctrl+→	One word to the right.
Ctrl+←	One word to the left.
Ctrl+↑	One paragraph up.
Ctrl+↓	One paragraph down.

continues

Table 4.1   Continued

Press	To Move
End	To the end of the current line.
Home	To the beginning of the current line.
PgUp	To the top of the screen.
PgDn	To the bottom of the screen.
Alt+PgUp	To the previous page.
Alt+PgDn	To the next page.
Ctrl+Home	To the beginning of the document.
Ctrl+End	To the end of the document.

Using Your Mouse

Using the mouse to move around in a document is more intuitive. To move the cursor with the mouse, perform any of the following steps:

- To move the cursor (insertion point) to a specific character, move the mouse pointer over the character and click the left mouse button.

- To see text on the previous page in a document, click on the Previous Page button below the vertical scroll bar. To see text on the next page, click on the Next Page button just beneath it (see Figure 4.2).

> **But Where's the Stuff I Just Typed?**
> Keep in mind that moving the cursor with the Previous or Next Page buttons, or with the scroll bars, *does not move the insertion point*. To move the insertion point with the mouse, you must click inside the document. Make sure you do that *before you start typing*, or what you type will appear wherever the insertion point is actually located.

- To see text that is before or after the visible part of the document, use the scroll bars (as described in the following section).

Using Scroll Bars

Some users find it easier to move around in a document using scroll bars, as shown in Figure 4.2. The horizontal scroll bar lets you scroll text from left to right across the screen. The vertical scroll bar lets you view text that has scrolled off the top or bottom of the screen.

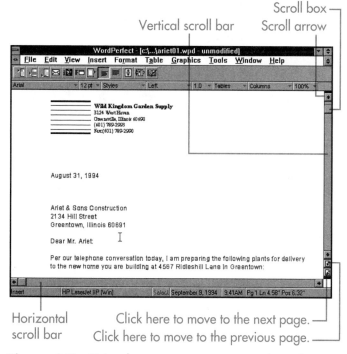

Figure 4.2 Using the mouse, you can move through a document quickly with the scroll bars, arrows, and buttons.

Perform any of the following steps to use a scroll bar:

- Click on the arrow at the end of the scroll bar to scroll up, down, left, or right one line or character at a time. To scroll continuously in the direction of the arrow, hold down the mouse button.

- Drag the scroll box in the scroll bar to move to the same relative location in the document. For example, if you drag the scroll box to the middle of the scroll bar, you will scroll to the middle of the document.

- Click inside the scroll bar, on either side of the scroll box, to scroll one screenful of text in the direction of the click. For example, if you click above the scroll box in the scroll bar, you'll see the previous screen of text.

- Click on the Previous Page or Next Page buttons on the vertical scroll bar to page through the document.

In this lesson, you learned how to type text and how to move around inside a document. In the next lesson, you'll learn how to edit your document by adding and deleting text.

Lesson

Editing Text

In this lesson, you'll learn how to insert text, type over existing text, and delete individual characters.

Inserting Text

You can insert text anywhere in a WordPerfect for Windows document. For example, you may want to insert a sentence in the middle of a paragraph or add a word to the beginning of a paragraph. To insert text, perform the following steps:

1. Move the cursor (insertion point) to the place where you want the text inserted.

2. Type the text. As you type, WordPerfect moves the existing text to the right and rewraps the text.

> **Mouse Mania** Remember that if you scroll through a document with the mouse, you must then click inside the document to move the insertion point (cursor).

Typing over Existing Text

WordPerfect starts in Insert mode; whatever you type is inserted at the cursor, and existing text moves to make room for the new text. If you want to replace text using Insert mode, you must first delete existing text and then type the new text.

However, sometimes it is faster to type over existing text. To type over text, perform the following steps:

1. Move the cursor to the beginning of the text you want to type over.

2. Press the Ins key to switch from Insert to Typeover mode. (The word **Typeover** appears on the Status Bar.)

3. Start typing. Each character you type replaces an existing character on-screen.

4. When you are finished typing over existing text, press the Ins key to switch back to Insert mode. (The word **Insert** reappears on the Status Bar.)

Tab Key Curiosity   In Typeover mode, the Tab key moves the cursor from one tab stop to the next without indenting text. If you want to use the Tab key to indent the first line of a paragraph, you must change back to Insert mode.

Mode Change   You can also double-click on the word **Insert** on the Status Bar to change to Typeover mode, and vice-versa.

Correcting Small Mistakes

In Lessons 6 and 7, you'll learn how to delete, copy, and move blocks of text to make sweeping changes to your document. However, to make minor corrections, you can delete individual characters or words by performing any of the following steps:

- Move the cursor (the blinking vertical line) to the left of the character you want to delete, then press Del.

- Move the cursor to the right of the character you want to delete, then press Backspace.

- To delete a word, move the cursor to the word you want to delete, then press Ctrl+Backspace.

- To delete from the cursor position to the end of a line, move the cursor to the place you want to begin deleting, then press Ctrl+Del.

Correcting Mistakes with QuickCorrect

QuickCorrect automatically corrects common typos as they happen; for example, it fixes typos like **adn** for "and," and **teh** for "the." You don't have to do anything to make this feature work; it is on by default. You can, however, customize QuickCorrect by adding additional words that you often misspell, along with their correct spellings.

To customize the QuickCorrect feature:

1. Open the Tools menu and select QuickCorrect, or press Ctrl+Shift+F1. The QuickCorrect dialog box appears, as shown in Figure 5.1.

Type a misspelled word. ⌐ Type a correction.

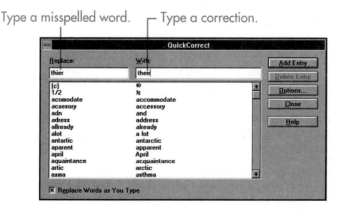

Figure 5.1 Customize QuickCorrect to your needs.

2. Under Replace, type a misspelled word.

3. Under With, type the correct spelling for that word.

4. Click on Add Entry.

5. **(Optional)** Repeat steps 2 to 4 to add additional words.

6. Make sure the option Replace Words as You Type is selected.

7. Click on Close to return to your document.

When you type a misspelled word, QuickCorrect automatically replaces it with the correct spelling. QuickCorrect also corrects other errors, such as two upper-case letters at the beginning of a sentence, and double-spacing between sentences. You can change these options by clicking on the Options button from within the QuickCorrect dialog box.

If you don't like QuickCorrect and you want to turn it off, select Tools/QuickCorrect or press Ctrl+Shift+F11. Deselect the Replace Words as You Type option, and click OK.

Undoing Your Changes

As you make changes to your text, WordPerfect stores your editing changes in a temporary holding area. You can restore changes from this holding area using Undo. For example, if you accidentally delete text and immediately realize your mistake, you can restore the text with Undo.

You can also undo other actions, not just deletions, using the Undo command. For example, if you moved a paragraph and immediately realized it shouldn't have been moved, you can use Undo to put it back where it belongs. You can undo your *last editing change* by performing either of the following:

- Open the Edit menu and select Undo.

  OR

- Click on the Undo button on the Toolbar.

  OR

- Press Ctrl+Z.

> **Undo Redo**   Undo the last Undo command by
> selecting Edit/Redo or by pressing Ctrl+Shift+R.

Undo stores your last ten changes to the document (but you can increase this number if you want). To restore older changes, follow these steps:

1. Open the Edit menu and select Undo/Redo History. The Undo/Redo History dialog box appears, as shown in Figure 5.2.

Changes listed above the one
you select will also be undone.

Figure 5.2   You can restore older changes with Undo/Redo History.

2. Select the last editing change you want to undo. Changes listed above the one you select will also be undone.

3. Click on Undo.

Once is Not Enough!   To increase the number of editing changes that WordPerfect tracks, click on the Options button in the Undo/ Redo History dialog box. Type a number (up to 300) and click OK.

In this lesson, you learned how to insert text, type over existing text, make minor changes to text, and undo your last editing actions. In the next lesson, you will learn how to select blocks of text for making bigger changes.

Lesson

Selecting Blocks of Text

In this lesson, you'll learn how to select blocks of text using the mouse or the keyboard.

Understanding Text Blocks

A text block is any amount of text that you select (highlight), in preparation for editing, as shown in Figure 6.1. Once you highlight a section of text, you can then perform some operation on the selected text, such as deleting or copying the text, changing the margins for the text block, or even making the text bold or italic. You'll learn about operations you can perform on text blocks in upcoming lessons.

You can select a text block with either the mouse or the keyboard, as explained in the following sections.

Selecting a Block with the Mouse

If you have a mouse, you can use the mouse to select (highlight) text by following these steps:

1. Click on the first character you want to mark.

2. Hold down the mouse button. This anchors the cursor.

3. Drag the highlight to the opposite end of the block and release the mouse button. The selected block appears highlighted, as shown in Figure 6.1.

Text block

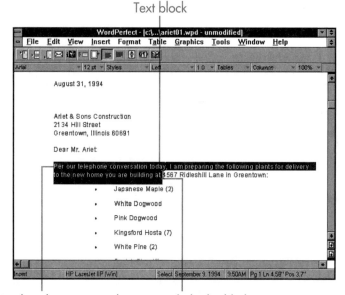

Anchor the cursor at the beginning of the text you want to mark.

Stretch the highlight to the opposite corner of the text.

Figure 6.1   A block of text.

Word Up!   As you highlight text, you'll notice that WordPerfect highlights entire words for you automatically. If you'd rather select text character by character instead of word by word, you can. Simply select Edit/Preferences, double-click on the Environment icon, then deselect Automatically Select Words.

Wrong Text?   If you want to unselect the highlighted text, simply click anywhere in the document or press an arrow key.

Selecting a Block with the Keyboard

To select a text block with your keyboard, perform the following steps:

1. Move the cursor to the beginning of the block you want to mark. This position is your pivot point, allowing you to stretch the highlight over the text.

2. Hold down the Shift key and move the cursor to the end of the text you want to block. You can use any of the cursor movement keys you learned about in Lesson 4.

3. Release the Shift key. You have marked your text so you can now perform a block operation on it; for example, you can press Ctrl+B to make the selected text bold.

Selecting a Sentence, Paragraph, or Page

Although stretching the highlight over text is the most precise way to select text, you may want to work with more logical units of text: sentences, paragraphs, and pages. For example, if you want to move a sentence from the end of a paragraph to the beginning, you can mark the sentence, cut it, and then paste it. Take these steps to select a sentence, paragraph, or page:

1. Move the cursor anywhere inside the sentence, paragraph, or page you want to select. (You can use the keyboard or mouse.)

2. Open the Edit menu and choose Select. The Select submenu appears, as shown in Figure 6.2.

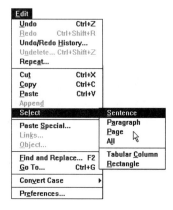

Figure 6.2 The Select submenu allows you to work with logical units of text.

3. Select Sentence, Paragraph, Page, or All. The sentence, paragraph, page, or entire document appears highlighted.

> **Such a Drag** You can use QuickSelect to select text without dragging. Double-click on a word to select it. Triple-click to select a sentence. To select a paragraph, double-click in the left margin in front of the paragraph.

The last two options on the Select submenu, Tabular Column and Rectangle, allow you to select text in vertical columns, rather than text that is wrapped (as in a paragraph). Their use is beyond the scope of this book, but you can experiment with them if you want.

In this lesson, you learned how to select text blocks. In the next lesson, you will learn how to delete, copy, and move text blocks in your document.

Lesson

Deleting, Copying, or Moving a Text Block

In this lesson, you'll learn how to delete, copy, and move marked blocks of text in a document.

What's the Difference?

To copy or move text, you use three commands: Cut, Copy, and Paste. These commands utilize an area in memory called the *Clipboard* that temporarily holds text while it is in the process of being moved or copied. Before you start copying or moving text, you should be familiar with the difference between these three actions:

Copy leaves the text block in the document and places an exact duplicate on the Clipboard, a common holding area used by all Windows-based programs.

Cut removes the text block from the document and places it on the Clipboard.

After text has been placed on the Clipboard by the Copy or Cut commands, you can then **Paste** the text block from the Clipboard into another document, somewhere else in the same document, or even into a document in another Windows-based program.

Text remains on the Clipboard even after you paste it, so you can paste a selection multiple times as needed. For example, if you want to repeat the words **Thank You!** several times in a letter, you can type it once, Copy it to the Clipboard, and then issue the Paste command as many times as you want. However, keep in mind that you can only place one item on the Clipboard at any one time. So if you later use the Copy command to copy the phrase **You're Welcome!**, it would replace the older **Thank You!** phrase on the Clipboard.

If you want to copy a block to the Clipboard without replacing the block that's already on the Clipboard, mark the block and then open the Edit menu and select Append. The block is tacked on to the end of the Clipboard's current contents.

It's Outta There   If you cut or copy another text block before pasting the first text block somewhere else, the second text block replaces the first on the Clipboard. You lose the first text.

Deleting a Text Block

In Lesson 5, you learned how to make small changes to a document with the Del and Backspace keys. However, deleting a paragraph or a page one character at a time can be time-consuming. To delete a section of text more quickly, take the following steps:

1. Mark the text block, as explained in Lesson 6.

2. Press the Del or Backspace key to delete the selected block.

Undeleting Text   To undelete text you've accidentally deleted, use the Undo command. For more information, refer to Lesson 5.

Copying a Text Block

When you copy text, the original text stays where it is, and WordPerfect places a copy of the text on the Clipboard so you can paste it wherever you want. To copy a text block, you can use either the mouse or the keyboard.

Copying a Text Block with the Mouse

Copying text with the mouse is probably the simplest method you can use:

1. Select the text you want to copy. See Lesson 6 for help.

2. Press and hold the Ctrl key.

3. Move the mouse pointer over the selected text and hold down the mouse button.

4. Drag the text to the desired location and release the mouse button and the Ctrl key. WordPerfect copies the text to the new location, as shown in Figure 7.1.

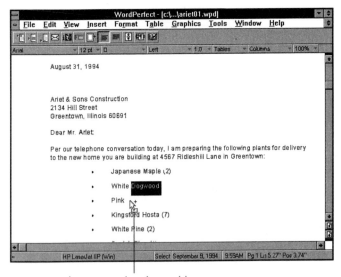

Drag the text to the desired location
and release the mouse button.

Figure 7.1 Copying text with the mouse is the easiest way.

Copying a Text Block with the Keyboard

1. Mark the text block you want to copy, as explained in Lesson 6.

2. Select Edit/Copy or click on the Copy button on the Toolbar.

3. Move the insertion point to the place in the document where you want to place the copied text. You can switch to another document if you want.

4. Select Edit/Paste or click on the Paste button on the Toolbar. WordPerfect pastes the copied text at the insertion point within the document.

Fast Copies   You can quickly copy text by
selecting it, pressing Ctrl+C to copy, then moving
the cursor and pressing Ctrl+V to paste the text.
You can also click the right mouse button, and
select Copy and Paste from the QuickMenu.

Moving a Text Block

When you move text, you remove the selected text from the
document and place it on the Clipboard. From there,
WordPerfect pastes it in a new location. To move a text
block, you can again use the mouse or the keyboard.

Moving a Text Block with the Mouse

Editing your document with the mouse is probably the
easiest method. To move text with the mouse, follow these
steps:

1. Select the text you want to move. See Lesson 6 for
   help.

2. Move the mouse pointer over the selected text and
   hold down the mouse button.

3. Drag the text to the desired location and release the
   mouse button. The text moves to the new location.

What Was I Doing?   It's easy to forget
whether you're in the middle of copying or
moving text when you use the mouse. To tell the
difference, just look at the mouse pointer. It
changes to a rectangle with a little plus sign when you're
copying. When you're moving text, it changes to just a
rectangle.

Moving a Text Block with the Keyboard

1. Mark the text block you want to move, as explained in Lesson 6.

2. Select Edit/Cut or click on the Cut button on the Toolbar.

3. Move the insertion point to the place in the document where you want to move the text. You can switch to another document if you want.

4. Select Edit/Paste or click on the Paste button on the Toolbar. WordPerfect moves the text to the location in the document marked by the insertion point.

> **Fast Moves**   You can quickly move text by selecting it, pressing Ctrl+X to cut, then moving the cursor and pressing Ctrl+V to paste the text. You can also click with the right mouse button and select Cut and Paste from the QuickMenu.

In this lesson, you learned how to delete, copy, and move text blocks in a document. In the next lesson, you'll learn how to save your work.

Lesson

Saving and Closing Documents

In this lesson, you'll learn how to save the document that you are working on to disk, and how to remove it from your screen so you can begin working on a new document.

Saving a Document to Disk

As you type, your computer's memory (RAM) holds your work. When you quit WordPerfect (or if the power to your computer is turned off), your computer erases your work. To store your work permanently, you must save it in a named *file* on a disk, such as your computer's hard disk, or a diskette.

Naming Files

When you enter the command to save a file, WordPerfect displays a dialog box that asks you to name the file. When naming a file, follow these file naming conventions:

- A file name consists of a base name (up to eight characters), a period, and an optional extension (up to three characters).

- You can use any characters in the base name and extension except the following:

  space + = | \ / < > , [ ] " : ; ? *

Here are some examples of valid file names:

CHAPTER8.DOC   OUR.DB   MARK'S.ADV

SALES_95.NET   P-AND-L.WK4   SALES.Q4

Here are some examples of invalid file names:

CHAP*8.DOC   MARK\PAT.DB   MAY94.WKSHT

SALES 95.NET   P/L.WK4   SALES:Q4

Saving a Document for the First Time

When you save a document for the first time, you must assign a file name to the document and tell WordPerfect where to store it on disk. Perform the following steps to save a file you have just created:

1. Select File/Save, or click on the Save button on the Toolbar. The Save As dialog box appears, as shown in Figure 8.1.

Type the file name here.   Click OK when done.

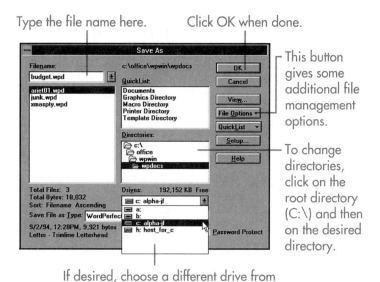

If desired, choose a different drive from the Drives drop-down list.

Figure 8.1   The Save As dialog box prompts you to name the file.

2. **(Optional)** If you do not want to store the file on the current drive, click on the down arrow under Drives and select another drive from the list.

> **Diskette Disco**   To save your document onto a diskette, select drive A or B in step 2.

3. **(Optional)** If you do not want to save your document in the default directory, change to a different directory in the Directories list box.

4. In the Filename text box, type a name for the file.

> **What's in a Name?**   WordPerfect uses the extension .WPD to identify documents you create. Be sure to use the extension .WPD when naming your file, as in PRMEMO.WPD.

5. Click OK. WordPerfect saves the document to disk.

After you save a document to disk, you can continue working on it if you want. Just be sure to *resave* your document after you make more changes. If you want to remove the document from the screen so you can work on other documents, see the "Closing a Document" section later in this lesson for help.

If you use other directories frequently to store certain files, you can add them to the QuickList. Just click on the QuickList button in the File Save As dialog box, and select Add Item. Change to the directory you want to add and type a description, such as Woodlands Project Files. Click OK. The directory now appears in the QuickList area of the dialog box. To change to your directory, select it from the list.

Saving Your Document Again

When you save a document, only its current contents are
saved to disk. If you add or delete text or change the document in some other way, those changes are only in your
computer's temporary memory. To prevent your changes
from getting lost, you should save your document again. It's
a good practice to save your document regularly during an
editing session. (Actually, WordPerfect saves your document
for you every 10 minutes, but it's a good idea to save a
document yourself before you make any major changes.) To
save a document that you have already named, perform one
of the following steps:

- Open the File menu and select Save.

  OR

- Click on the Save button on the Toolbar.

  OR

- Press Ctrl+S.

The Save As command on the File menu (F3) is similar
to the Save command, but it lets you save a copy of the
current file using a different file name or location, among
other options. Rather than just *resaving* the document, the
File/Save As command reopens the Save As dialog box for
your use. With it, you can then create a copy of your document to edit (by giving it another name), and leave your
original file intact.

Changing the Default Directory

When you save a file in WordPerfect, it automatically saves
that file to a directory called WPDOCS, which is under the
main \OFFICE\WPWIN directory. If you have a directory to
which you regularly save your files, you may want to change
this default, so you won't have to change the drive and
directory every time you save or open a file:

1. Open the Edit menu and select Preferences. The Preferences dialog box appears, as shown in Figure 8.2.

File icon

Figure 8.2   The Preferences dialog box.

2. Double-click on the File icon. The File Preferences dialog box appears, as shown in Figure 8.3.

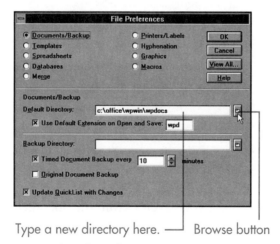

Type a new directory here. —┘   └ Browse button

Figure 8.3   The File Preferences dialog box.

3. Click on the Documents/Backup option.

4. Type a new directory in the Default Directory text box. If you want to browse the available drives and directories, click on the Browse button to the right of the text box. It's okay to type the name of a directory that does not exist; WordPerfect will create it for you.

5. Click OK. The Preferences dialog box reappears.

6. Click on Close to return to your document.

Closing a Document

Even though you can have several documents open at once, you will find that closing documents you no longer need on-screen makes WordPerfect for Windows run more efficiently. To close a document, perform these steps:

1. Select File/Close, or press Ctrl+F4. If you've modified the document, a dialog box appears asking if you want to save your changes before exiting (see Figure 8.4).

Figure 8.4 WordPerfect reminds you to save your work before closing a document.

2. Select Yes. If you haven't saved the document before, the Save As dialog box opens and you must follow the steps under the section "Saving a Document for the First Time." If you have saved the document previously, WordPerfect saves it again and then closes the document.

Quick Close   You can also close a document by double-clicking on its Control-menu box, located in the upper left-hand corner of the document window (just under a larger Control-menu box, which you can use to close down WordPerfect).

In this lesson, you learned to save and close Word-Perfect documents. In the next lesson, you'll learn to find and open them.

Lesson

Retrieving Documents

In this lesson, you'll learn how to locate WordPerfect documents on your disk and open them.

Opening a Document

When you save a document, you save it in a file on disk. To make changes to a document later on, you must open its file; the document then appears on-screen where you can work on it. Perform the following steps to open a document file:

1. Select File/Open, or click on the Open button on the Toolbar. The Open File dialog box appears (see Figure 9.1).

Select a file to open from the list.   Change to a different drive or directory if you want.

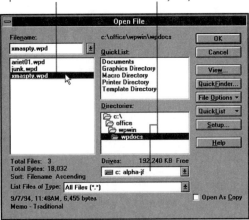

Figure 9.1   The Open File dialog box.

2. **(Optional)** If the file you want to open is on a
different drive, use the Drives drop-down list.

3. **(Optional)** If the file you want to open is not in the
default directory, change to a different directory in
the Directories list box.

4. Select the file you want to open from the Filename
list. If you want to open more than one file at a
time, simply press Ctrl as you click on each file
name.

> **Little Lost File** If you're having trouble locating
> the right file, the QuickFinder can help you. See
> the next section for details. You can also view a
> file before opening it; see the "Viewing a Docu-
> ment Before You Open It" section for more information.

5. Click OK. WordPerfect opens a new document
window for each document you select. To switch
between open documents, press Ctrl+F6 or select
the document you want to move to from the Window menu.

WordPerfect remembers the names and locations of the
last four files you worked on. They appear at the bottom of
the File menu. Reopen any recently edited file by simply
selecting it from this list.

If you frequently store certain files in other directories,
add them to the QuickList. Just click on the QuickList button
in the File Save As dialog box, and select Add Item. Change
to the directory you want to add, and type a description,
such as Woodlands Project Files. Click OK. The directory
now appears in the QuickList area of the dialog box. To
change to your directory, select it from the list.

Working with Multiple Open Documents

If you already have a document open and you open another one, your original document stays open. However, you may not be able to see your original document because it's underneath the just-opened document.

To move between open document windows, press Ctrl+F6 or open the Windows menu and select the document you want to move to. You can also use the Cascade, Tile Vertical, or Tile Horizontal commands on the Window menu to make it easier to organize and view the separate documents. Cascade arranges the open document windows so their title bars are neatly stacked; Tile arranges the windows so you can see the contents of each.

Switching Windows When windows are tiled or cascaded, you can click anywhere inside the desired window to switch to it.

Earlier, you learned about cutting, copying, and pasting using the Clipboard. You can cut, copy, and paste between document windows as easily as within the same document; simply move your cursor to the second document window before you issue the Paste command. For more information, turn back to Lesson 7.

If you're done with your original document, close it before opening another one. This keeps your screen from becoming cluttered, and enables your PC to work faster. To close a document, select File/Close or press Ctrl+F4.

Finding Documents

The QuickFinder helps you if you forget where you've saved an important file and can't remember the name of the file. QuickFinder enables you to search through multiple directories, and even drives, to find the misplaced file.

Using QuickFinder

1. From within the Open File dialog box, click on
QuickFinder. The QuickFinder dialog box appears,
as shown in Figure 9.2.

Enter text to search for, or a filename pattern.

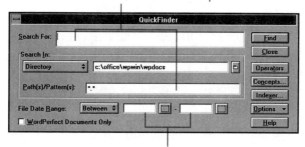

Enter a range of dates if you want.

Figure 9.2   The QuickFinder dialog box helps you locate
files.

2. Enter the information that you know about the file:

- If you are sure that the file contains a certain
  text string, such as "Dear Mrs. Fulton," enter
  it in the Search For text box.

- If you know the file's name, or part of its
  name, indicate it in the Path(s)/Pattern(s) text
  box. Use wild cards if needed. For example, if
  you are sure that the file begins with MM and
  has a WPD extension, enter MM*.WPD in the
  Path(s)/Pattern(s) text box.

Wild Cards   Wild cards are symbols that you
can use in a file name to represent characters
you don't know. An asterisk (*) stands for any
number of characters, and a question mark (?)
stands for a single character.

- If you want to restrict the search to WordPerfect files only, select the WordPerfect Documents Only check box.

- If you want to restrict the search to files that you last changed on or around a particular date, enter those dates in the File Date Range.

3. (Optional) Choose Search In and specify whether WordPerfect should search the current directory, the entire disk, or a subdirectory (subtree). If you choose Disk, a drop-down list of available disk drives appears so you can choose.

4. Click on Find. The search begins. If WordPerfect finds any files that match your specifications, they will appear in a Search Results List dialog box (shown in Figure 9.3).

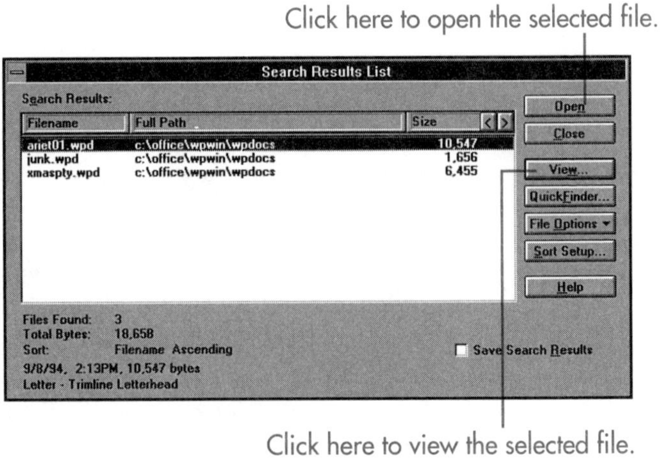

Click here to open the selected file.

Click here to view the selected file.

Figure 9.3   QuickFinder search results.

From the Search Results List dialog box, you can highlight a file and choose Open to open it or View to examine the file before opening it. To return to the Open File dialog box without opening a file, click on Close.

Viewing a Document Before You Open It

Before you open a document, you can view it to be sure that it is the correct one. Follow these steps:

1. From the Open File dialog box, select a file to view.

2. Click on View. The Viewer window opens to display the contents of the file you selected, as shown in Figure 9.4.

Select another file to view from this list.

Control-menu box

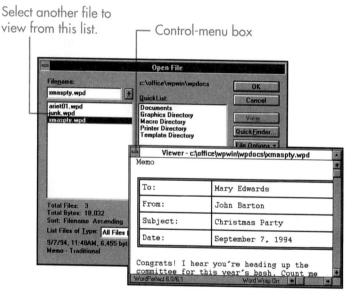

Figure 9.4   The Viewer window lets you see the contents of your files.

3. Perform some action:

   - To see other parts of the viewed file, use the scroll bars in the Viewer window.

   - To view another file, select it from the Filename list in the Open File dialog box.

- To change some of the Viewer options, click with the right mouse button in the Viewer window, and select an option from the QuickMenu.

- To open the file you're viewing, click OK in the Open File dialog box.

- To close the Viewer window without doing anything, double-click on its Control-menu box.

In this lesson, you learned how to find and open a file. In the next lesson, you will learn how to preview your document before printing it and how to print a paper copy of your document.

Lesson

Printing Your Document

In this lesson, you'll learn how to select a printer, view your document on-screen before you print it, and print a single copy of your entire document.

Selecting a Printer

Most Windows-based programs use the printer driver that you installed during your Windows installation. WordPerfect gives you the option of choosing between the Windows printer driver and its own printer support. If you use mostly Windows, choose the Windows printer driver. However, if you share your documents with co-workers who use a variety of environments, such as Windows, OS/2, and DOS, you may want to select the WordPerfect printer driver so that your document prints correctly on all PCs.

> **Driver** Special program that controls an optional computer device, such as a printer, modem, or CD-ROM drive.

Whether you decide to use the Windows or the WordPerfect printer driver, you should select a printer before you start working on a document in WordPerfect. That way, what you see on-screen will look the same as your printed document.

You can choose from among all the printers you've installed through Windows plus all the printers you installed during your WordPerfect installation. Follow these steps:

1. Select File/Print, or click on the Print button on the Toolbar. The Print dialog box appears.

2. Click on Select. The Select Printer dialog box appears, as shown in Figure 10.1.

Click here to select the Windows default printer driver.

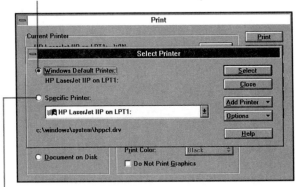

Click here to select other printer drivers.

Figure 10.1   Use the Select Printer dialog box to choose the printer driver you want to use.

3. Select a printer to use:

   • To select the default Windows printer driver, click on the Windows Default Printer option.

   • To select a WordPerfect printer driver or a different Windows driver, select one from the Specific Printer drop-down list.

4. Click on Select. The Print dialog box reappears.

5. Click on Close to return to your document.

The printer you chose is now the default printer for all documents. You do not need to select a printer for other documents unless you want to change the printer on which you want to print a particular document.

What's Next, Doc?   Now that you have the correct printer chosen, return to your document to preview it before printing. See the next sections for help.

Previewing Your Document (Zooming In)

There are several ways to see how your document will look before you print it.

Draft View

Although you can edit your document in Draft view, it does not appear as it will when printed. (Draft mode does not show the entire page layout, such as the headers or footers. See Lesson 2 for more information.) Switch to Page or Two Page view using the View menu to preview your document before printing.

Page View and Zoom Options

WordPerfect's Page view displays your document as it will look when printed (see Lesson 2 for help changing views). By changing the Zoom, you can zoom back and view the entire page, or zoom in and examine details close up. To change the Zoom:

1. Select Zoom from the View menu. The Zoom dialog box appears (see Figure 10.2).

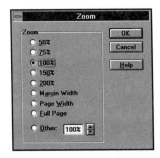

Figure 10.2 The Zoom dialog box.

2. Click on an option or type a percentage next to Other. (Margin Width displays just the text but not the margins; Page Width displays the document with blank space for the margins; and Full Page reduces the document so you can see an entire page.)

3. Click OK. The view changes to the selected zoom percentage.

> **Go Zoom** You can change the zoom quickly by clicking on the Zoom button on the Power Bar, then selecting a zoom option.

You can switch to Page view and Full Page zoom in one stroke by clicking on the Page/Zoom Full button on the Toolbar. This button toggles between the current view and Full Page zoom/Page view.

Two Page View

WordPerfect's Two Page view works well for previewing print jobs, too. It allows you to see how two pages will look side by side, which is useful when planning two-sided publications. To use this view, select Two Page from the View menu.

Printing Your Document

You have many options when you print a document; you can print only certain pages, print multiple copies, and so on. However, first you need to learn how to print a single, complete document—one copy, no frills.

1. Select File/Print or click on the Print button on the Toolbar. The Print dialog box appears, as in Figure 10.3.

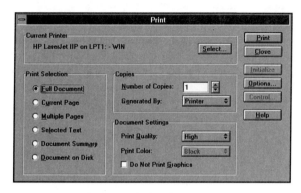

Figure 10.3   The Print dialog box.

2. Click on Print. WordPerfect prints one copy of your document.

> **Printer Problems**   If your printer does not start printing, make sure your printer is on, has paper, and is *online* (most printers have a light that shows when the printer is online).

Make It Fit!   You can force your document to
fit on a specified number of pages with Make It
Fit. Select Format/Make It Fit Expert or click on
the Make It Fit button on the Toolbar. Enter the
number of desired pages, and select the items you want
WordPerfect to adjust (such as line spacing, margins,
and so on) in order to make the document fit into the
desired number of pages. Finally, click on Make It Fit.

In this lesson, you learned how to select a printer
driver, preview before printing, and print your document. In
the next lesson, you will learn how to print selected pages or
multiple copies of your document. You will also learn how
to print envelopes.

Lesson

Advanced Printing Options

In this lesson, you'll learn how to print selected pages or multiple copies of your document. You'll also learn how to create a matching envelope and print it.

Printing Selected Pages

If you want to print only selected pages of your document, follow these steps:

1. Select File/Print or click on the Print button on the Toolbar. The Print dialog box appears (see Figure 11.1).

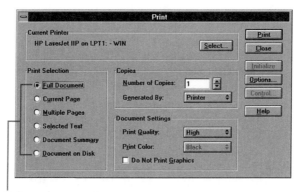

Select what to print.

Figure 11.1 The Print dialog box offers many advanced features.

2. Select the pages to print:

- To print the current page only, click on Current Page.

- To print selected pages, click on Multiple Pages.

3. Click on Print. If you selected Multiple Pages, the Multiple Pages dialog box appears, as shown in Figure 11.2.

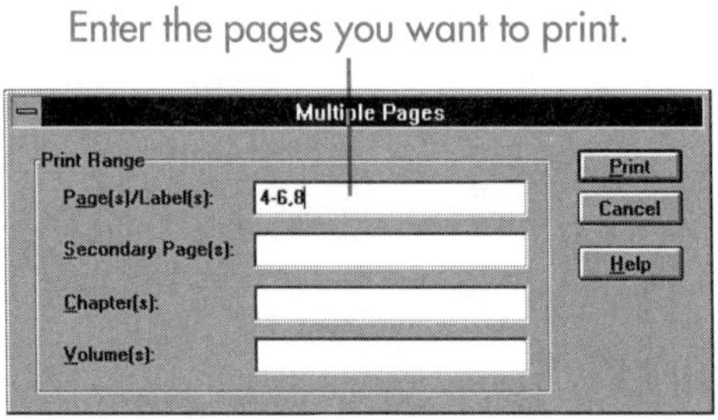

Enter the pages you want to print.

Figure 11.2   The Multiple Pages dialog box.

4. (Optional) If you selected Multiple Pages to print, under Page(s)/Label(s), enter the pages to print:

- To print only page 4, type 4.

- To print pages 4, 6, and 8, type 4,6,8.

- To print from the beginning of the document to page 4, type -4.

- To print from page 4 to the end of the document, type 4-.

- To print pages 4 to 6, type 4-6.

- To print pages 4 to 6 and 8, type 4-6,8.

5. Click on Print. WordPerfect prints the selected pages.

If you want to print selected text instead of selected pages, just select the text you want to print, click on the Print button on the Toolbar, then click on Print.

Printing Multiple Copies

You can have WordPerfect print multiple copies of your document and save time at the copier. To print multiple copies:

1. Select File/Print or click on the Print button on the Toolbar. The Print dialog box appears (see Figure 11.1).

2. Under Number of Copies, type the number of copies you want.

3. Click on Print. WordPerfect prints multiple copies of your document.

> **Reverse That!** If your printer ejects the pages face-up, then the last page of your document ends up on top. This is annoying, especially when you're printing multiple copies of a document. Try this instead: click on the Options button in the Print dialog box, select Print in Reverse Order (Back to Front), and click OK. Page one will print last and end up at the top of the print pile.

Printing Envelopes

It's easy to print an envelope to go with your letter:

1. Open the Format menu and select Envelope. The Envelope dialog box appears, as shown in Figure 11.3.

Verify the recipient's address.

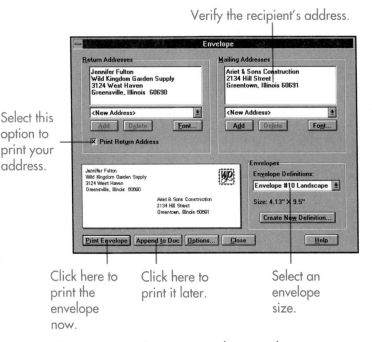

Select this option to print your address.

Click here to print the envelope now.

Click here to print it later.

Select an envelope size.

Figure 11.3 Printing a matching envelope is easy.

2. (Optional) If necessary, under Return Addresses, type your address. (You'll only need to do this once, the first time you use the Envelope feature.)

> **No Deposit, No Return** If you don't want your return address to print (for example, you're using preprinted envelopes), click on Print Return Address to deselect it.

3. (Optional) If necessary, under Mailing Addresses, make changes to the recipient's address. (WordPerfect picks up this address from your letter, so you probably won't need to make any adjustments to it.)

Fancy Font   You can click on the Font button and change the font (the typeface) for both the Return and Mailing addresses.

4. Under Envelope Definitions, select an envelope size.

5. Select a print option:

   • To print the envelope now, click on Print Envelope.

   • To print the envelope when you print the letter, click on Append to Doc.

In this lesson, you learned how to print selected pages, print multiple copies of your document, and print envelopes. In the next lesson, you will learn how to change the way your text looks.

Lesson 12

Changing the Look of Your Text

In this lesson, you'll learn how to change the appearance of your text by changing its font (typeface) and by adding attributes, such as bold, italics and underlining.

What Is Character Formatting?

When you start typing a document, whatever you type appears in plain text. If you want to set off a section of the text or emphasize a word or phrase, you can enhance the text by changing its *formatting*. Character formatting affects how text looks, just as paragraph formatting (alignment, indentation, and so on) affects how a paragraph appears. (You'll learn more about paragraph formatting in upcoming lessons.)

To change the formatting of text, you change its *font* or add an attribute, such as bold, italics or underlining. Figure 12.1 depicts various fonts and attributes.

Font   A family of text that shares the same design and size. For example, Times New Roman 12-point is a font. Times New Roman is the design (or typestyle) and 12-point is the size (there are 72 points in an inch).

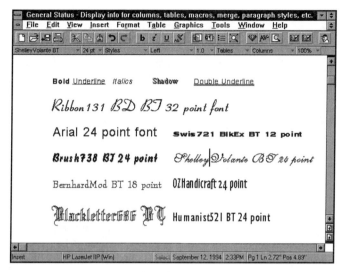

Figure 12.1   Examples of several common fonts and attributes.

Changing the Font, Size, or Attributes of Text

You can change the formatting of existing text, or you can format text as you type. To format existing text, first select it, then select the formatting options you want. To format text as you type, first select the formatting options you want, type your text, then turn the formatting options *off*. Follow these steps:

1. **(Optional)** To format existing text, select it. (See Lesson 6 for help.)

2. Select Format/Font or press F9. The Font dialog box shown in Figure 12.2 appears.

So Many Choices!   You can also display the Font dialog box by clicking with the right mouse button and selecting Font from the QuickMenu.

Select a font face and font size.   Select the attributes you want.

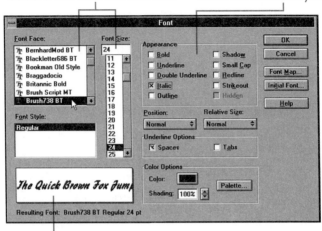

A sample appears here.

Figure 12.2   Select an attribute from the Font dialog box.

3. Select a Font Face and/or Font Size. The sample changes to reflect your choices.

4. Choose the attributes you want from the Appearance section of the dialog box.

5. Click OK.

6. (Optional) If you're formatting text as you type, type the text now. Then repeat steps 2–5 to turn the attributes off.

> **Quick Attributes**   There are shortcut keys that you can use instead of the Font dialog box to make text bold, italic, and underlined. Simply press Ctrl+B for bold, Ctrl+I for italic, and Ctrl+U for underline. Use these same key combinations to turn the attributes off later on, if you are formatting as you type.

If you want to change selected attributes, such as the font size but not the font, you may find it faster to use the Power Bar instead of the Font dialog box. In addition, you can apply other attributes quickly with the Toolbar. Read the "Applying Attributes with the Power Bar and the Toolbar" section for more help.

Changing the Default Font

By default, WordPerfect uses the font Times New Roman 12-point for all new documents. You can change this for one document, or for all new documents if you want. Follow these steps:

1. Open the Format menu and select Document.

2. Click on Initial Font. The Document Initial Font dialog box appears, as shown in Figure 12.3.

Fast Font   You can also display the Document Initial Font dialog box by clicking on the Initial Font button in the Font dialog box shown in Figure 12.2.

Select a font face and font size.

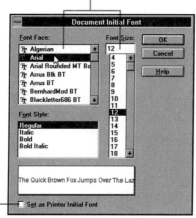

Click here to set this font for all documents.

Figure 12.3   Change the default font with this dialog box.

3. Select a Font Face and/or Font Size.

4. **(Optional)** To change the default font for all documents and not just the current one, select Set as Printer Initial Font.

5. Click OK. Any existing text whose formatting you did not override appears in the font you selected. New text will also use this default font.

Applying Attributes with the Power Bar and the Toolbar

The Toolbar and the Power Bar make it easy to change selected attributes of your text, as shown in Figure 12.4.

Change font face and font size with the Power Bar.

Change common attributes with the Toolbar.

Recently used fonts appear at the top of the Font Face list.

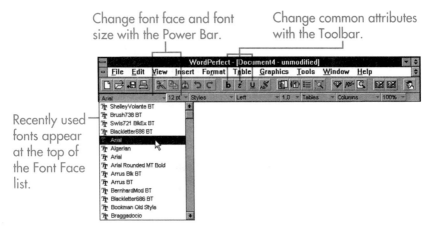

Figure 12.4 Use the Toolbar and the Power Bar to change text quickly.

To format text with the Power Bar or the Toolbar, follow these steps:

1. **(Optional)** To format existing text, select it.

2. Click on the appropriate button on the Toolbar or
the Power Bar.

3. If necessary, select an option (such as the font size)
from the Power Bar drop-down list.

4. **(Optional)** Type your text; then turn the attribute
off by repeating steps 2 and 3.

More Power   You can customize the Power Bar or
the Toolbar to include buttons for other text attributes
you often use. See Help for more details.

Copying Attributes to Other Text

Once you have some text formatted the way you like, you
can copy its formatting onto other text with QuickFormat.
Just follow these steps:

1. Select the text whose formatting you want to copy.

2. Select Format/Quick Format or click on the
QuickFormat button on the Toolbar. The
QuickFormat dialog box appears, as shown in
Figure 12.5.

3. Select an option:

* To copy the character formatting of the
selected text, choose Characters.

* To copy the paragraph formatting (margins,
alignment, and so on) of the selected text,
choose Headings. (You'll learn more about
paragraph formatting in upcoming lessons.)

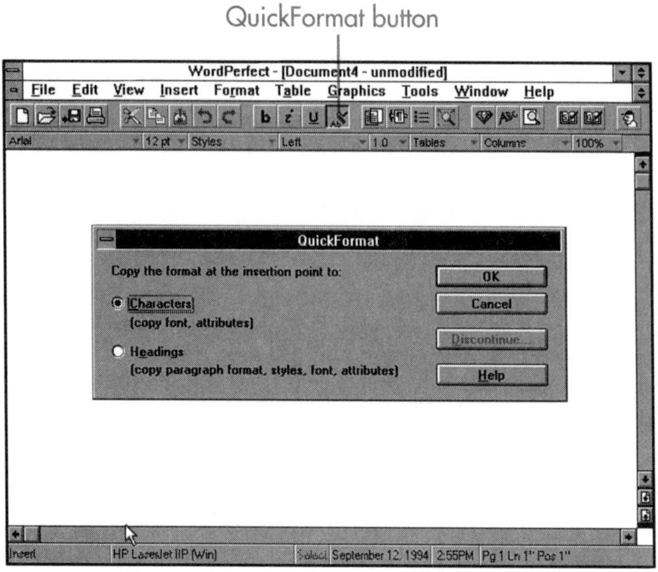

QuickFormat button

Figure 12.5 Copy the formatting of selected text to other text.

4. Click OK. The cursor changes to a tiny paintbrush.

5. Drag the cursor over the text you want to change. Repeat for additional text.

6. Select Font/QuickFormat or click on the QuickFormat button on the Toolbar to turn off QuickFormat and return the cursor to normal.

Text formatted with QuickFormat is *linked* to the original text, so that changes to the original text are automatically copied to the QuickFormatted text.

In this lesson, you learned how to enhance text by applying attributes to the text. In the next lesson, you will learn how to view and work with the attribute codes.

Lesson

Working with WordPerfect Codes

In this lesson, you'll learn how to view the codes that WordPerfect uses to control your document and how to work with those codes.

What Are WordPerfect Codes?

In the previous lesson, you enhanced text by changing its font, making the text bold or italic, or assigning the text some other attribute. Whenever you enhance text, WordPerfect inserts two invisible formatting codes: one that turns the attribute on and another that turns it off. These codes work in the background to control the appearance of your text.

WordPerfect adds the following three types of codes to documents:

- **Paired codes** WordPerfect uses paired codes to surround text in a particular attribute, such as bold or italic. The attribute in question affects only the text between the two codes. For example, to bold the phrase "How's this for emphasis?" WordPerfect would place a pair of hidden codes around it, as in **[Bold]How's this for emphasis?[Bold]**.

- **Open codes**   WordPerfect uses open codes for paragraph and page settings that take effect from the code to the end of the document. For example, if you changed the line spacing in the middle of the document from single- to double-space, WordPerfect inserts one code: **[Ln Spacing:2.0]**. That code affects all the text that follows it, unless you enter another line spacing code later on (where you change the line spacing back to single, for example).

- **Single codes**   WordPerfect uses single codes to mark changes that affect only the current position, such as pressing Enter, in which case, WordPerfect inserts the code **[HRt]** (for hard return).

Why Worry About Codes?   Normally, you don't have to think about the hidden codes; they do their work in the background. However, if your text looks funny on-screen or in print, or if your margins are not turning out as you expect, you can view the codes to find the cause of the problem and correct it.

Revealing Hidden Codes

You're probably wondering what these codes look like. To view the codes, display the Reveal Codes screen (like the one shown in Figure 13.1) by performing one of the following:

- Press Alt+F3.

  OR

- Open the View menu and select Reveal Codes.

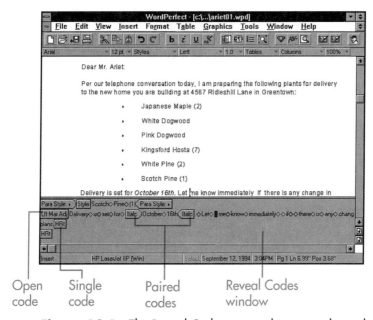

Figure 13.1   The Reveal Codes screen shows you the codes that control your text.

With Reveal Codes turned on, the screen splits in two; normal text appears in the top part of the screen, and the text with codes appears in the lower part. You can type, edit, and format your document as you normally would, but now you can work with the codes as well.

To hide the Reveal Codes window, press Alt+F3 or select View/Reveal Codes again.

Removing Codes

Once you display the codes, you can edit them to change the look and layout of your text. In most cases, editing consists of deleting the code. For example, if you want to unbold some text, you can delete either the Bold On or Bold Off code. (You only have to delete one code because the bold attribute is controlled by a pair of codes; deleting one of them deletes the pair.) To delete a code, perform the following steps:

1. Press Alt+F3 to turn on Reveal Codes if it's not already on.

2. Click on the code you want to remove.

3. Press the Del key to delete the code.

Fast Deletion You can also delete a code by dragging it out of the Reveal Codes window.

Changing Open Codes

If you want to change the settings put in place by an open code (for example, the line spacing), perform the following steps:

1. Double-click on the code in the Reveal Codes window. For example, double-click on **[Ln Spacing:2.0]**. The normal dialog box for that option appears.

2. Make your changes as you normally would within the dialog box.

3. Click OK.

In this lesson, you learned how to display WordPerfect's hidden formatting codes, delete codes, and change open codes. In the next lesson, you'll learn how to create bulleted and numbered lists.

Lesson 14

Creating Numbered or Bulleted Lists

In this lesson, you'll learn how to add numbered or bulleted lists to your documents.

Why Use a List?

A list is useful for highlighting important information for a reader. You've seen many examples of bulleted and numbered lists in this book. Specifically, a bulleted list is good for items that do not have a specific order, such as a shopping list (see Figure 14.1). A numbered list, on the other hand, is helpful when describing steps for completing a specific task, or for listing items in the order of importance, as in a Top Ten list.

Creating a List

WordPerfect comes with many bulleted and numbered list styles from which you can choose. To create a list:

1. Open the Insert menu and select Bullets & Numbers. The Bullets & Numbers dialog box appears, as shown in Figure 14.2.

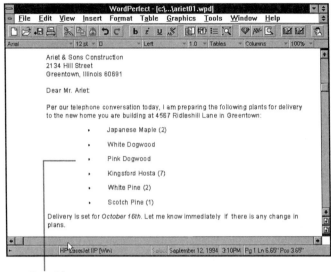

Bulleted list

Figure 14.1 A bulleted list is useful for items that do not have a specific order.

Select a bulleted or numbered list style.

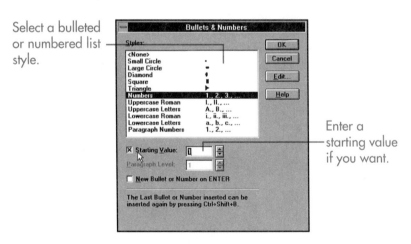

Enter a starting value if you want.

Figure 14.2 The Bullets & Numbers dialog box provides many choices.

2. Select a bulleted or numbered list style from the Styles list.

3. **(Optional)** To change the starting number in a numbered list, click on Starting Value and type a number.

4. Click OK.

5. Type the text for the first item and press Enter.

6. To add an additional item, press Ctrl+Shift+B or click on the Insert Bullet button on the WordPerfect Toolbar.

Faster Than a Speeding Bullet   To quickly create a bulleted or numbered list, click with the right mouse button and select Bullets from the QuickMenu.

Adding Items to a List

Adding additional items to the end of a list is easy, but what if you have to add an item in the middle of a list? Follow these steps:

1. Move the insertion point to the item directly *below* the place you want to insert a new item.

2. Press Enter to insert a new line.

3. Press Ctrl+Shift+B or click on the Insert Bullet button on the WordPerfect Toolbar. WordPerfect automatically renumbers the list to reflect the new item (see Figure 14.3).

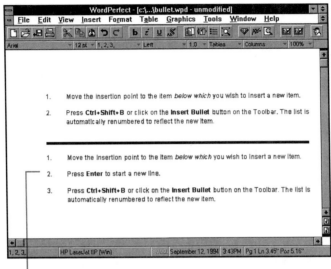

When a new item is added,
WordPerfect automatically
renumbers the list.

Figure 14.3 Adding a new item to a list is easy.

In this lesson, you learned how to create bulleted or numbered lists. In the next lesson, you'll learn how to set the tabs for a document.

Lesson

Setting Tabs

In this lesson, you'll learn how to set and clear tab stops in WordPerfect.

What Are Tabs?

Whenever you press the Tab key in a document, WordPerfect moves the cursor (and any text that's to the right of the cursor) to a tab stop. Unless you specify otherwise, tab stops are set at half-inch intervals from the left margin. So, if you press the Tab key once, the cursor moves one-half inch in (to the right) from the left margin. Press Tab again, and the cursor moves another half-inch interval to the right.

Viewing the Tab Stop Settings

Your current tab settings appear on the Ruler Bar if you have displayed it. If you have not displayed the Ruler Bar, turn it on now by opening the View menu and selecting Ruler Bar, or by pressing Alt+Shift+F3. The tab settings appear as triangles, as shown in Figure 15.1.

Types of Tab Stops

Initially, all tab stops are left tab stops; that is, any text you type at the tab stop aligns flush left against the stop. You can change the type of tab stop to center the text, right-align it, or align a decimal point on the tab stop (for aligning a column of numbers). Figure 15.1 shows the various types of tab stops and how you can use them.

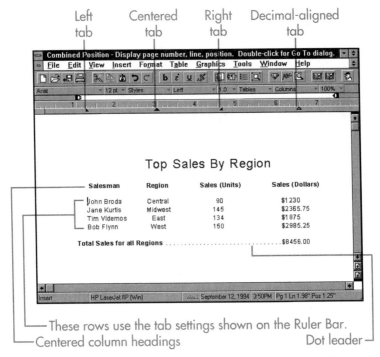

These rows use the tab settings shown on the Ruler Bar.
Centered column headings   Dot leader

Figure 15.1   Text aligns differently depending on the type of tab stop.

Dot Leader   A special character (such as a period or a hyphen) that fills the blank space between tab settings in a columnar list.

Clearing Tab Stops

The tab stop ruler can easily become cluttered with tab stop settings. If you need to use only two or three tab stop settings, you may want to clear some before you add more. There are several ways to clear tab stop settings.

The easiest way to clear a single tab stop setting is to click on its marker on the Ruler Bar and drag the tab stop *downward* off the Ruler.

To clear all of the tab stop settings, it's easier to use the Clear All Tabs option than to drag each one off the Ruler individually. Follow these steps:

1. Move the cursor to the beginning of the paragraph whose tab stop settings you want to clear, or start a new paragraph. To clear tabs for a single paragraph, select it now.

2. Click on the tabs area of the Ruler with the right mouse button. A QuickMenu appears.

3. Select Clear All Tabs from the menu.

See the next section for help in adding the tab settings you want.

Adding Tab Stops

After clearing away the tab settings you don't need, you can add new ones. To add tab settings with the Ruler:

1. Move the cursor to the beginning of the paragraph whose tab stop settings you want to set, or start a new paragraph. To change the tab settings for a single paragraph instead of the rest of the document, select it now.

2. **(Optional)** To change the current tab type, click with the right mouse button on the tabs area of the Ruler and select a different tab type from the QuickMenu.

3. To set a tab, click on the Ruler below the numbered scale. A tab set of the current tab type appears on the Ruler where indicated.

If you prefer, you can set tab stops from the Tab Set dialog box instead. This option takes more time but offers greater control. Follow these steps:

1. Move the cursor to the beginning of the paragraph whose tab stop settings you want to clear, or start a new paragraph. To change the tab settings for a single paragraph instead of the rest of the document, select it now.

2. Open the Format menu, select Line, then select Tab Set to display the Tab Set dialog box (see Figure 15.2).

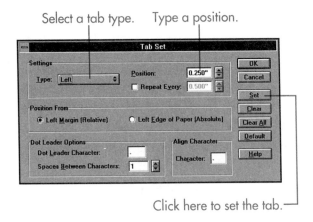

Figure 15.2 Set precise tabs with the Tab Set dialog box.

3. Select the tab type you want from the Type list.

4. **(Optional)** To set tabs based on their distance from the left edge of the paper rather than the left margin (the default), select Left Edge of Paper (Absolute).

5. Type the distance (from either the left margin, or the left edge of the paper) at which you want the new tab stop to appear in the Position text box.

6. (**Optional**) Type a new dot leader character and adjust the spaces between characters if you want.

7. Click on Set to set the tab.

8. Repeat steps 3 through 7 for any additional tab stops you want to set.

9. Click OK.

Repeating Tabs   In the Tab Set dialog box, there is a Repeat Every option. Use this feature to set evenly spaced tab stops across the entire Ruler Bar without setting each one individually.

Get a Move On   To move a tab stop, click on it and drag it along the Ruler. To delete a tab stop, drag it *downward* off the Ruler.

In this lesson, you learned how to align text by changing tab stop settings. In the next lesson, you will learn how to change the line spacing and change the alignment of text in other ways.

Lesson

16

Setting the Line Spacing and Justification

In this lesson, you'll learn how to change the line spacing for an entire document or a portion of it, and how to align text between the left and right margins.

Changing the Line Spacing

As you type, WordPerfect single spaces the text. Sometimes, however, you may want to double space or triple space your text. For example, you may want to leave extra space between lines to write comments when reviewing a report.

You can change the line spacing for an entire document or a section of it by performing the following steps:

1. Move the cursor to the point within the document where you want the line spacing to change. To change the line spacing for the entire document, move the cursor to the top of the document by pressing Ctrl+Home.

> **Selected Text** To change the line spacing for a single paragraph or any text block, select the text block.

2. Open the Format menu and select Line. Select Spacing. The Line Spacing dialog box appears (see Figure 16.1).

Figure 16.1   The Line Spacing dialog box lets you enter a line spacing setting.

3. Type the desired line spacing setting. (You can type a decimal entry to add line spaces between each line; for example, type 2.5 to add 2.5 line spaces between each line.)

4. Click OK.

Speedy Spacing   Click on the Line Spacing button on the Power Bar to quickly change line spacing.

If you want to change the line spacing later in the document, simply move to where you want the line spacing to change and repeat steps 1 through 4.

To return to the original line spacing setting, remove the line spacing code. Press Alt+F3 to turn on Reveal Codes, then remove the Ln Spacing code you just inserted by dragging it out of the Reveal Codes window (see Lesson 13).

Justifying Text: Left, Right, Full, or Center

As you type text, WordPerfect justifies (*aligns*) the text against the left margin, leaving the lines uneven at the right. You can change the justification (alignment) of text to *center* it, *right-justify* it (align it against the right margin), or *fully justify* the text so each line is flush against both the left and right margins (see Figure 16.2). All and Full justification are the same except that Full leaves the last line of a paragraph unjustified, while All justifies everything.

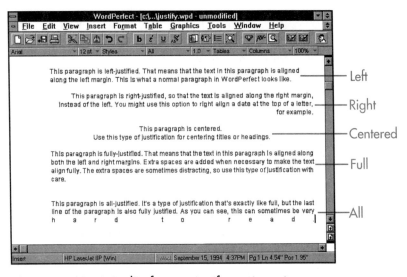

Figure 16.2   WordPerfect can justify text in various ways.

You can change the alignment of text at any point in a document—for a single line, or for a text block. The following sections explain how.

Justifications   WordPerfect refers to the various text alignment options as *justifications*.

Changing Justification in a Document

When you change the justification of text, it changes from that point until the end of the document, unless you change the justification later on in the document. If you want to change the justification of only a certain section of text, select that section before you change the justification.

Perform the following steps to change the justification:

1. Move the cursor to the point where you want the justification to change. If you want to change only a specific section of text, select it now.

2. Click on the Justification button on the Power Bar, or select Format/Justification.

3. Select the desired justification.

Shortcuts   There are shortcut keys for all of the justification options except All. Press Ctrl+L to left justify selected text, Ctrl+R to right justify it, Ctrl+E to center text, and Ctrl+J to fully justify text.

Centering a Page   You can center text vertically on a page (on a title page, for example) if you want. Open the Format menu, select Page, then select Center. Click on the desired centering option (Current Page or Current Page and Subsequent Pages), then click OK.

Indenting Text

An *indent* is added space between the margin and the edge
of a paragraph. You add an indent to increase the space
between the left or right edge of a paragraph and the margin.
For example, you may want to indent a list or a long quote to
set it off from regular text. WordPerfect provides you with
three options for indenting text: left indent, double indent,
and hanging indent (see Figure 16.3).

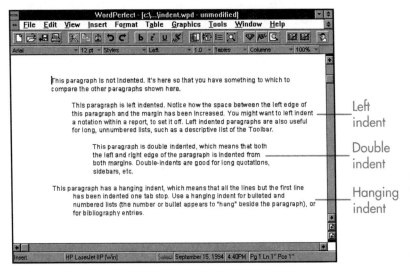

Figure 16.3 WordPerfect's indentation options.

Indenting a Single Paragraph

To indent a single paragraph, perform the following steps:

1. Move the cursor to the first character of the paragraph you want to indent. Do not select (highlight)
   any text, or it won't work.

2. Open the Format menu and select Paragraph. A submenu opens that includes the indentation options.

3. Select the desired indent option: Indent, Double Indent, or Hanging Indent. WordPerfect indents the text as specified.

Quick Indents   Instead of steps 2 and 3, you can use shortcut keys to indent a paragraph. Use F7 for a left indent, Ctrl+F7 for a hanging indent, and Ctrl+Shift+F7 for a double indent. In addition, there's an Indent button on the Toolbar that you can click to add a left indent (but it's only visible when you move the Toolbar into the work area).

If you decide later that you do not want the text indented, delete the Indent code. A quick way to delete the Indent code is to move the cursor to the first character in the paragraph and press the Backspace key. You can also turn on Reveal Codes (Alt+F3) and delete the Indent code by dragging it out of the Reveal Codes window.

Indenting Multiple Paragraphs

To indent multiple paragraphs at the same time, use the Ruler:

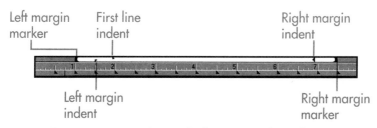

Figure 16.4   Indent multiple paragraphs at the same time with the Ruler.

1. Select the paragraphs whose indentation you want to change.

2. Drag the appropriate indent marker along the Ruler, then release the mouse button. The selected paragraphs will indent.

For example, to left indent a paragraph, select it, then click on the left indent margin marker on the Ruler. Drag the marker along the Ruler to the desired location, then release the mouse button. All the lines of the paragraph will indent the same amount. To indent only the first line of a paragraph, select it and press Ctrl. Click on the first line indent marker and drag. When you release the mouse button, only the first line of the selected paragraph indents.

> **Proper Indentation**   To left indent a paragraph, click on the left indent marker and drag. To indent the first line only, press Ctrl and drag just the first line indent. To create a hanging indent, first indent the paragraph with the left indent marker, then press Ctrl and drag the first line indent marker back towards the left margin.

In this lesson, you learned how to change the line spacing and text justification and how to indent text. In the next lesson, you'll learn how to enter paper size and margin settings for your document.

Lesson

17

Setting the Paper Size and Margins

In this lesson, you'll learn how to specify the size of the paper you want to print on and how to change the margins for an entire document or a portion of it.

Selecting the Paper Size and Type

Unless you choose otherwise, WordPerfect assumes you want to print on standard 8.5-by-11-inch paper in portrait orientation. If you want to print on a different size paper or in landscape orientation (sideways on a page), you must select a different paper size and/or type.

Orientation Orientation refers to how the printer prints text on the page. *Portrait* prints the text parallel to the short side of the page; *landscape* prints the text parallel to the long edge, making a printed page wider than it is long, as in 11-by-8.5-inch paper.

Paper Type Paper type refers to the kind of paper used, such as letterhead, envelope, labels, or transparency.

You can change the paper size for the entire document
or for a selected portion. For example, if you have a report
that you want to print in portrait orientation on 8.5-by-11-
inch paper, followed by a chart that you'd like to print in
landscape orientation on 14-by-11-inch paper, select a
different paper size and type just for the chart. Perform the
following steps:

1. Move the cursor to the point within the document
   where you want to change the paper size. To
   change the paper size for the entire document,
   move the cursor to the top of the document by
   pressing Ctrl+Home.

2. Open the Format menu and select Page. A submenu
   appears.

3. Select Paper Size. The Paper Size dialog box appears, as shown in Figure 17.1.

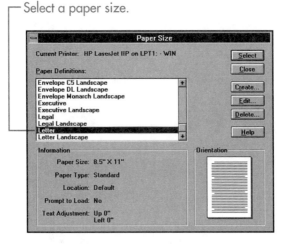

Figure 17.1 The Paper Size dialog box enables you to tell
WordPerfect what size and type of paper you are using.

4. Choose the paper that you want to print on from the Paper Definitions list. A paper definition includes both size and type. The Information box shows the specifications for the selected paper definition.

5. Choose Select when you're done.

> **Just Your Size**   You can also display the Paper Size dialog box by clicking on the Paper Size button on the Toolbar. (Warning: this button only appears when you move the Toolbar into the work area.)

Creating or Changing a Paper Definition

You can create your own paper definitions or edit an existing one. For example, you can create a paper definition for printing on 5.5-by-8-inch paper (standard day-planner paper). Follow these steps:

1. Open the Format menu and select Page. A submenu appears.

2. Select Paper Size. The Paper Size dialog box appears, as shown in Figure 17.1.

3. To change an existing paper definition, select it and click on Edit. Otherwise, click on Create. Either the Edit Paper Size or Create Paper Size dialog box appears.

4. Complete the definition and make changes as necessary (see Figure 17.2).

Set the paper size here.
Choose a paper type here.
If you are defining a new paper definition, type its name here.

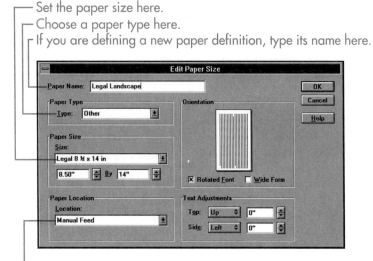

Choose the paper tray to use, if your printer has more than one.

Figure 17.2   Change a paper definition with the Edit Paper Size dialog box.

Keep these things in mind as you create or edit a paper definition:

- If you're defining a new paper definition, you'll need to type a name for it in the Paper Name text box.

- Select Rotated Font if you want to change between portrait and landscape orientation.

- Select Wide Form if you want to feed the paper into the printer wide-end first.

- To indent the entire document text an additional amount from the margins, use the Text Adjustments area. For example, to move the text downward another inch from the top of the page (to make room for a preprinted header, for example), set the Top (Down) adjustment to 1 inch.

5. Click OK to return to the Paper Size dialog box.

6. Click on Select to select the paper definition for the current document.

Setting the Page Margins

Unless you choose otherwise, WordPerfect uses a 1-inch margin, setting text 1 inch from the left, right, top, and bottom edges of the page. You can change any of these margins for any portion of a document by performing the following steps:

1. Move the cursor to the point within the document where you want the margins to change. To change the margins for the entire document, move the cursor to the top of the document.

> **Setting the Left and Right Margins for Selected Text** To change the left and right margins for selected text, select the text you want to change in step 1. To change the margins for a single paragraph, you really just add an indent (extra space between the paragraph and the document margins). See Lesson 16 for help.

2. Open the Format menu and select Margins, or press Ctrl+F8. The Margins dialog box appears (Figure 17.3).

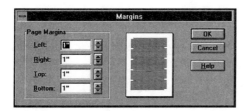

Figure 17.3 The Margins dialog box enables you to set top, bottom, left, and right margins.

3. Type the new setting (in inches) for the margin(s) you want to change.

4. Click OK.

> **No Margins for Error**   You can also display the Page Margins dialog box by clicking on the Page Margins button on the Toolbar. (Warning: this button only appears when you move the Toolbar into the work area.)

Changing the Margins with the Ruler

You may find it easier to change the margins with the Ruler. To display the Ruler, open the View menu and select Ruler, or press Alt+Shift+F3. Then follow these steps:

1. Move the cursor to the point within the document where you want the margins to change. To change the margins for the entire document, move the cursor to the top of the document.

2. Click on the appropriate margin marker (see Figure 17.4).

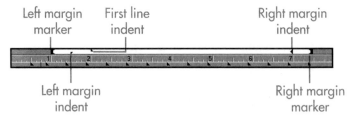

Figure 17.4   Changing margins with the Ruler is easy.

3. Drag the marker to the desired location and release the mouse button. The margins will change.

Marker Mania   To change the margins for a document, use the Left or Right margin marker. Use indent markers (Left, First line, and Right) to indent selected paragraphs an additional amount from the margin. See Lesson 16 for help with indents.

In this lesson, you learned how to specify the size and type of paper on which you intend to print, and how to change the left, right, top, and bottom margins for a document or for selected sections. In the next lesson, you'll learn how to work with styles to format a document.

Lesson 18

Working with Styles

In this lesson, you'll learn how to use styles to automatically format a section of text.

What Is a Style?

A *style* is a set of specific formats for a section of text, such as a heading, a salutation, or a report title. Once you create a style, you can apply that style to any section of text you want.

Using styles saves you time in formatting a document. For example, you can create a Heading style and use it to format all the headings in a report. In addition, if you make changes to the Heading style later on, all of the headings will change automatically for you!

WordPerfect has two types of styles:

Character style You can apply this type of style to any amount of text, from one character to several paragraphs. It includes specifics for how the text should look, such as the font, point size, and text attributes, such as bold or italics.

Paragraph style You can apply this type of style to whole paragraphs only, and not smaller sections of text, such as a word. It includes specifics on how the paragraph should look, such as the margin settings, line spacing, indents, tab settings, justification, or borders for a paragraph. It also includes character attributes, such as font and point size.

Applying a Style to Text

WordPerfect comes with several built-in styles that you can use, or you can create your own. Once a style exists, you can apply it to text by following these steps:

1. Select the text or paragraph to which you want to apply the style.

2. Click on the Styles list on the Power Bar to open it (see Figure 18.1).

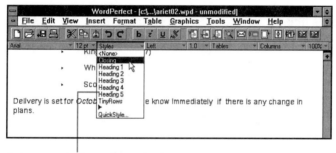

Select a style from the Styles list.

Figure 18.1   Use the Styles list to apply styles to text.

3. Select a style from the list. WordPerfect applies the style to the selected text.

The style name appears on the Power Bar in the Styles area whenever the insertion point is within the selected text.

Getting Rid of a Style   To remove a style from text, click on the Styles list on the Power Bar and select <None>.

Creating a Style

The easiest way to create a style is to format text the way
you want it and then copy that format into a style. Here's
how:

1. Format a section of text the way you want. For
example, format one heading the way you want all
your headings to look.

2. Open the Format menu and select Styles, or press
Alt+F8. The Styles List dialog box appears.

3. Click on QuickStyle. The QuickStyle dialog box
appears, as shown in Figure 18.2.

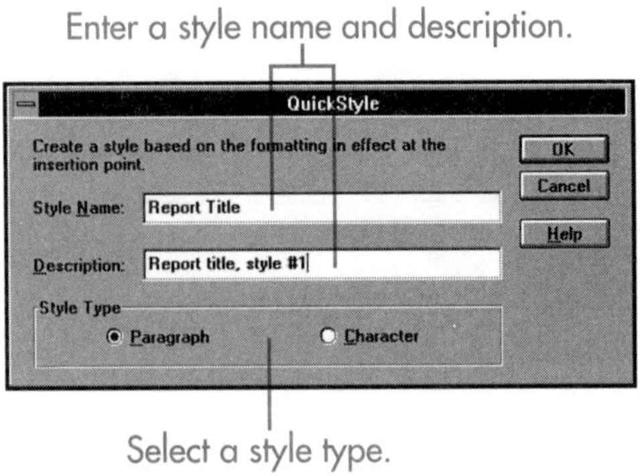

Enter a style name and description.

Select a style type.

Figure 18.2 The QuickStyle dialog box.

4. Next to Style Name, type a name for your style,
such as **Report Title**.

5. **(Optional)** Next to Description, type a description
for the style.

6. Select Paragraph (to create a paragraph style) or
Character (to create a character style).

7. Click OK. The Styles List dialog box reappears.

8. Click on Apply. WordPerfect applies the style to the selected text, and the style name appears in the Styles list on the Power Bar.

Quicker QuickStyle   You can also display the QuickStyle dialog box by selecting QuickStyle from the Styles list on the Power Bar.

Making Changes to a Style

To make changes to a style, follow these steps:

1. Move the insertion point to a section of text that has the style you want to change.

2. Make changes to that text. Other sections of text in that style will update automatically.

What Happened?   Your changes didn't update? Your style must be nonautomatic. See the next section for help.

When you create a paragraph style using QuickStyle, it's marked as "auto," which means that when you make changes to text in that style, other text in the same style is automatically changed. The default WordPerfect styles are not automatic, so you must change them manually by selecting Apply from the Styles list as described previously.

Making a Style Nonautomatic

Sometimes, you don't want a paragraph style you create to be "automatic," because you may not want one simple change to affect all the other paragraphs in that same style. To change a paragraph style so that it *isn't automatic*:

1. Open the Format menu and select Styles. The Style List dialog box appears.

2. Select the style you want to change.

3. Click on Edit. The Styles Editor dialog box appears, as shown in Figure 18.3.

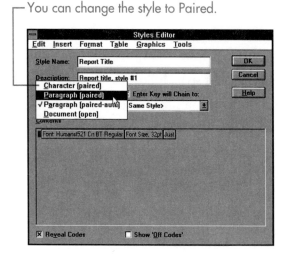

Figure 18.3   The Styles Editor dialog box.

4. Select Paragraph (paired) from the Type list.

5. (Optional) Make any other changes you want.

Formatting Déjà Vu   Use the menus (just as you would to format regular text) to add additional formatting options to this style. To delete an option, drag it out of the Contents box.

6. Click OK. The Styles List dialog box reappears.

7. Click on Close.

Saving Your Styles for Reuse

When you create a style, it is normally saved within the current document. That means that if you want to reuse that style in another document, you must create it all over again. If you want, you can save your styles in a *style library* for reuse.

> **Style Library**   A file that contains a set of styles that you have saved for reuse. For example, you can save a set of styles in a file called NEWSLTR.STY and reuse the styles in every newsletter you create.

Follow these steps to save your styles in a style library:

1. Open the Format menu and select Styles. The Styles List dialog box appears.

2. Click on Options.

3. Select Save As. The Save Styles To... dialog box appears.

4. Type a file name (such as **NEWSLTR.STY**) for your library. (Be sure to use the extension **.STY**.)

5. Select User Styles.

6. Click OK. WordPerfect saves the styles you've defined in the current document for reuse.

7. Click on Close to close the Style List dialog box.

To open your style library in a new document so you can reuse your styles, just select Format/Styles, then click on Options. Select Retrieve and type in the name of your style library. Click OK, and the styles are copied into the current document. (You may need to switch directories to find your styles, if you saved them in a special directory originally.)

Lesson

Adding Headers and Footers

In this lesson, you'll learn how to add text that appears at the top or bottom of every page in your document.

What Are Headers and Footers?

A *header* is text that appears at the top of every page of a document. For example, this book includes a header that displays the page number, lesson number, and lesson title. A *footer* is just like a header except that it appears at the bottom of every page.

The left-hand header in this book is slightly different than the right-hand header (one displays the lesson number and the other displays the lesson title). WordPerfect allows you to create separate left-hand and right-hand headers and footers, too.

Too Much Work? You don't have to add headers or footers if all you want to do is number your pages. See Lesson 20 for more help.

Where'd They Go? Headers and footers do not display in Draft mode. Switch to Page or Two Page mode (on the View menu) to see headers and footers.

Creating a Header or Footer

To create a header or footer, follow these steps:

1. **(Optional)** Open the View menu and select Page or Two Page view. (You can't see headers and footers in Draft view.)

2. Move the cursor to the first page on which you want the header or footer to appear.

3. Open the Format menu and select Header/Footer. The Headers/Footers dialog box appears (see Figure 19.1).

Figure 19.1   The Headers/Footers dialog box.

4. Select Header A or Footer A. You can make two of each (A or B) to create different left-hand and right-hand headers or footers, but start with A for now.

5. Click on Create. The title bar changes to indicate that you're editing a header or a footer, and not the main document. A feature bar also appears at the top of the editing window, as in Figure 19.2.

Feature Bar   WordPerfect displays an extra "bar" called a feature bar to help you work with specific features, such as table formulas, graphics, outlines, and headers and footers.

The window title bar shows that
you're editing a header or footer.

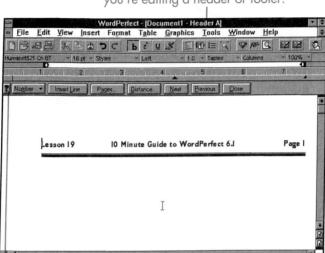

Header/Footer feature bar

Figure 19.2 A feature bar appears to help you edit your header or footer.

6. Type the text that you want to use for the header or footer. (You can type up to one page of text, but usually you type only one or two lines.)

7. Use the feature bar to include other features, such as page numbering. Table 19.1 explains what each button on the feature bar accomplishes.

8. When you finish entering your header or footer, click on the Close button on the feature bar. You return to editing the main document.

Where Is It?   If you're working in Draft view when you create or edit a header or footer, a separate window will open up for the header or footer. You can't see them on the page in Draft view, so they're shown in a window.

Table 19.1   Buttons on the Header/Footer feature bar.

Button	Function
Number	Inserts page numbers or other numbering.
Insert Line	Inserts vertical or horizontal graphic lines.
Pages	Specifies on which page (left, right, or both) the header or footer will appear. Use this option to create different left-hand and right-hand headers or footers.
Distance	Specifies how far from the text the header or footer is.
Next	Moves to the next header or footer in the document.
Previous	Moves to the previous header or footer in the document.
Close	Closes the Header/Footer feature bar.

Editing a Header or Footer

If you decide to change your header or footer later, you can edit it by performing the following steps:

1. Open the Format menu and select Header/Footer.

2. Select the header or footer you want to edit from the Headers/Footers dialog box (see Figure 19.1).

3. Click on Edit. The Header/Footer feature bar appears at the top of the editing window.

4. Make your changes.

5. Click on the Close button on the feature bar.

Turning Off a Header or Footer

After a certain point in the document, you may want to turn off the header or footer. For example, you may not want it to appear in the index or on the charts at the end of a report. To turn a header or footer off for part of a document, perform the following steps:

1. Move the cursor to the first page at which you want the header or footer discontinued.

2. Open the Format menu and select Header/Footer.

3. Select the header or footer that you want to discontinue.

4. Click on Discontinue. The header or footer discontinues on this page and any remaining pages within the document.

Just One Page   To suppress a header or footer for a single page (such as the title page), open the Format menu and select Page, then select Suppress. In the dialog box that appears, select the header or footer you want to suppress. Click OK.

Lesson 20

More Page Formatting

In this lesson, you'll learn how to force a page division and have WordPerfect automatically number the pages in your document. You'll also learn how to add a page border or fill, and add a drop cap.

Forcing a Page Break

As you type a document, WordPerfect automatically divides the document into pages based on the current page length and margin settings. As you add or delete text, WordPerfect redivides the text as needed into pages.

Sometimes, you want to divide the text into pages yourself. For example, you may want a large table to appear on a page by itself. In such a case, you can insert a hard page break (HPg) hidden code in the document by performing the following steps:

1. Move the cursor to the place in the document after which you want to create a page break.

2. Select Insert/Page Break or press Ctrl+Enter. WordPerfect inserts a HPg code at the cursor position and moves the following text onto a new page.

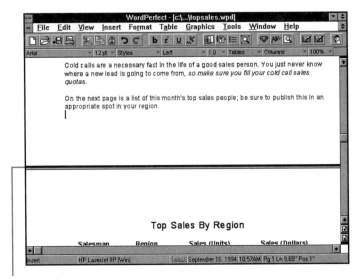

Page break

Figure 20.1   A soft or hard page break appears as a "gap" in Page view.

To remove a hard page break, move to the last character on the page before the page break, then press Delete.

Telling WordPerfect to Number the Pages

In Lesson 19, you learned how to add headers and footers to your document and how to insert a code in a header or footer that automatically inserts the correct page number. If all you want to print is a page number (with little or no accompanying text, a date, or special graphics), then you do not need to go to the trouble of adding a header or footer. WordPerfect supplies a much simpler way to number pages, as explained in the following steps:

Disappearing Act   Like headers and footers, automatic page numbers do not appear in Draft view. Use Page or Two Page view instead.

1. Move the cursor to the top of the first page on which you want page numbers to appear.

2. Open the Format menu and select Page. A submenu appears.

3. Select Numbering. The Page Numbering dialog box appears (see Figure 20.2).

Choose a page numbering position.

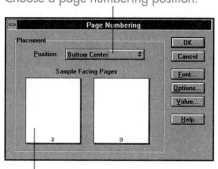

Sample pages show how your selection will appear.

Figure 20.2 The Page Numbering dialog box prompts you to specify your page number preferences.

4. Open the Position list and choose a page numbering position.

5. **(Optional)** To add some text in front of the number, such as the word "Page," click on Options and enter the text in the Format and Accompanying Text box. Click OK to return to the Page Numbering dialog box.

6. **(Optional)** To change the starting value (from page 1 to 2, for example), click on Value. Enter the starting number in the New Page Number text box. Click OK to return to the Page Numbering dialog box.

7. Click OK.

Adding a Page Border or Fill

To set off a title page, a page with important figures, or a chart, add a page *border* or *fill*. You also can place a border or fill around individual paragraphs instead of an entire page.

> **Border**   Placed in the margins of a page, a page border surrounds text. You also can place a border around a paragraph.
>
> **Fill**   Placed behind text, a fill acts as shading to set off important information.

To add a border or fill to a page:

1. Move the cursor to the first page in the document on which you want to place a border or fill.

2. Open the Format menu and select Page. A submenu appears.

3. Select Border/Fill. The Page Border dialog box appears, as shown in Figure 20.3.

Select a border style here.

	Page Border	
Border Options		OK
Border Style: [ ] Heavy Double ⬍		Cancel
Customize Style...		Off
		Help
Fill Options		
Fill Style: [ ] Waves ⬍		
Foreground: [ ] Background: [ ]		
☒ Apply border to current page only		

Click here to apply the border to this page only.   └ Select a fill style here.

Figure 20.3   Add interest to a page with a border or fill.

4. **(Optional)** Select a Border Style. To prevent this border from appearing on subsequent pages, click on Apply border to current page only.

5. **(Optional)** Select a Fill Style. Change the Foreground and/or Background colors to adjust the fill pattern.

6. Click OK.

To place a border or fill around specific paragraphs (instead of an entire page), select the paragraphs you want to change. Open the Format menu and select Paragraph. Select Border/Fill. A dialog box similar to the one shown in Figure 20.3 appears. Follow the previous steps to add a border or a fill.

Adding a Drop Cap

Although this is not a page feature, a drop cap adds interest to the top of the page. With the drop cap feature, you can enlarge the first letter or word of a paragraph. Drop caps add interest and a professional look to your documents, and they are easy to create:

1. Move the cursor to the paragraph to which you want to add a drop cap.

2. Open the Format menu and select Drop Cap, or press Ctrl+Shift+C. The Drop Cap feature bar appears, as shown in Figure 20.4.

3. **(Optional)** Customize your drop cap with the feature bar. Table 20.1 contains a description of each option.

4. Click on the Close button on the feature bar to return to your document.

Drop Cap feature bar

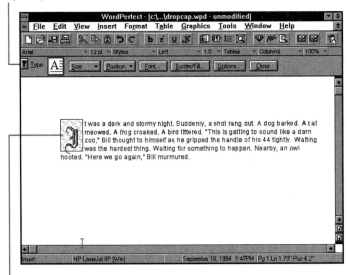

Drop cap, complete with a new font, border, and fill

Figure 20.4 Adding a drop cap.

Here's a brief description of each feature bar option.

Table 20.1 The Drop Cap feature bar.

Feature Bar Button	Function
Type	Select from several predefined drop cap styles.
Size	Change the size of the drop cap.
Position	Adjust the exact position of the drop cap.
Font	Change the font of the drop cap.

Feature Bar Button	Function
Border/Fill	Add a border and/or a fill to the drop cap.
Options	Select from several options, such as the number of characters to include in the drop cap.
Close	Close the Drop Cap feature bar and return to your document.

In this lesson, you learned how to force a page break in a document and how to use WordPerfect's page numbering feature. You also learned how to add borders, fills, and drop caps. In the next lesson, you'll learn how to place text in columns.

Lesson

Creating Columns

In this lesson, you'll learn how to arrange text into columns.

Why Use Columns?

You can use columns to arrange text in newsletters, brochures, booklets, annual reports, and more. Columns add visual impact to your documents and make text easier to read.

WordPerfect supports two different kinds of columns: *newspaper* and *parallel*. Newspaper columns are also called *snaking* columns, because the text "snakes" from the bottom of one column to the top of the next, as in a newspaper. Parallel columns place text in columns side by side, as in a table. You can use parallel columns in a report with a wide left margin where you place comments, as shown in Figure 21.1.

In addition, WordPerfect offers *balanced* newspaper columns and parallel columns with *block protect*. In balanced newspaper columns, when text does not fill a page, WordPerfect arranges the text so that the last lines in each column appear even. Parallel columns with block protect cause text in each column to flow together from page to page. (This is a good option to use if you want to be sure that your comments in the parallel columns stay next to the paragraph they refer to, as shown in Figure 21.1.)

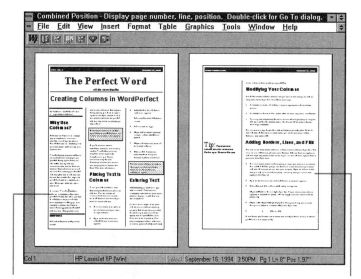

Newspaper columns   Parallel columns

Figure 21.1   WordPerfect offers two different types of columns.

Table Talk   If you want to create a short (one page) list with parallel columns, use a table, as described in Lesson 22.

By the Way   If you're about to create a newsletter, brochure, or something similar, WordPerfect has some templates that may help. Templates are "pre-formed" documents complete with formatting, to which you add text and graphics as needed. See Lesson 3 for more information.

Placing Text in Columns

When you define columns, WordPerfect places text in columns from that point forward. You can change the number of columns or even turn them off later in a document if you want. To create columns:

1. Move the cursor to the place in the document where you want to begin columns.

2. Open the Format menu and select Columns. A submenu appears.

3. Select Define. The Columns dialog box appears (see Figure 21.2).

Select the number of columns you want.

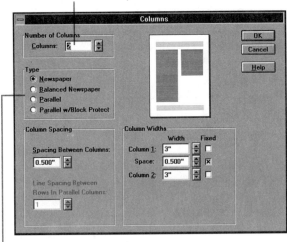

Select a column type.

Figure 21.2 The Columns dialog box.

4. Select the Number of Columns desired.

5. Select a column Type.

6. (Optional) Adjust the spacing between columns (called the *gutter*).

7. **(Optional)** Adjust the width of individual columns.

8. Click OK. Text in the document from that point forward is placed in columns.

> **Quick Columns**   You can create columns quickly by clicking on the Columns Define button on the Power Bar and selecting an option.

Entering Text into Columns

After creating your columns, type text as normal. When text in a newspaper style column reaches the bottom of a page, it flows into the next column.

To force text to begin in the next column, insert a column break by pressing Ctrl+Enter. This is useful for switching to the next column when you are typing text in a parallel list, or to force text to the beginning of the next newspaper column. After text is entered, press Alt+← or Alt+→ to move from column to column in a parallel list.

Modifying Your Columns

The Ruler contains column markers you can use to change the column and gutter widths (see Figure 21.3). Just follow these steps:

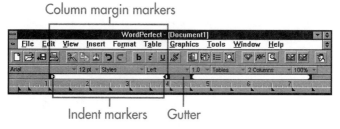

Column margin markers

Indent markers   Gutter

Figure 21.3   Use the Ruler to make adjustments to your columns.

- To change the width of a column, drag the appropriate column margin marker.

- To change the location of the gutter, click on it and drag it to a new location.

- To change the indentations for the current or selected paragraphs, drag the left, right, or first line indent marker. See Lesson 16 for more help with indenting paragraphs.

You can return to regular text (one column) without the help of the Ruler. To turn columns off later on in the document, open the Format menu, select Columns, then select Off.

Adding Borders, Lines, and Fills

You can add borders around columns, or lines between columns. You can even add a fill (shading) behind text. Borders, fills, and lines are applied to columns beginning at the cursor; however, you can turn off these options later in your document. Just select Format/Columns, then Border/ Fill. Select a border and/or fill style and click OK. For more help with borders or fills, see Lesson 20.

Between the Lines To place lines between columns, choose the Column Between Border Style.

In this lesson, you learned how to create and modify columns. In the next lesson, you'll learn how to create tables.

Lesson

Working with Tables

In this lesson, you'll learn how to create and format tables.

What Is a Table?

In most word processing programs, including WordPerfect, you can create columns of text by using tabs. However, if you have several columns of data of varying lengths, getting all the columns to align can be a chore. An easier way to create a table is to use WordPerfect's Table feature. See the sample WordPerfect for Windows table in Figure 22.1.

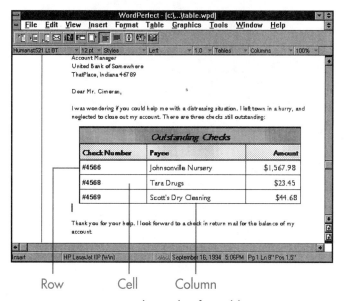

Figure 22.1 A typical WordPerfect table.

Rows, Columns, and Cells   As Figure 22.1 shows, a table consists of a series of *rows* and *columns* that intersect to form boxes called *cells*. You type text in the cells to form your table.

Creating a Table

Creating a basic table is easy; just tell WordPerfect the number of rows and columns you want, and WordPerfect does the rest. To create a basic table, perform the following steps:

1. Press Enter to start a new paragraph for your table.

2. Open the Table menu and select Create, or press F12. The Create Table dialog box appears (see Figure 22.2).

Enter the number of rows and columns you want.

Figure 22.2   Specify the desired number of rows and columns.

3. Enter the number of Columns you want in the table.

4. Enter the number of Rows you want.

5. Click OK. WordPerfect creates the table and displays it in your document.

Timely Tables   Create a table quickly by clicking on the Table QuickCreate button on the Power Bar and dragging to select the number of rows and columns you want.

Moving Around and Typing Text in a Table

To move around in a table, use the mouse to click inside a cell, or use the cursor movement keys, as described in Table 22.1. Once in a cell, you can type and format text just as you normally would. As you type text in a cell, the cell wraps the text and expands as needed.

Table 22.1   Table movement keys.

To Go	Press
One cell right	Tab
One cell left	Shift+Tab
One cell down	Alt+↓
One cell up	Alt+↑
First cell in row	Home, Home
Last cell in row	End, End
Top line of multiline cell	Alt+Home
Bottom line of multiline cell	Alt+End

Changing the Table's Size and Appearance

Although you can leave the table as it is, you may want to tinker with it by adjusting the width of the columns or the height of the rows, adding rows or columns, removing lines or adding shading, or applying other formats to the table.

Fast Track   The easiest way to format a table is to use the buttons on the Tables Toolbar, which normally appears whenever you click inside a table. If you don't want to use the Tables Toolbar, remember to use the QuickMenu, which contains table commands. Just right-click the mouse button when the cursor is over a table to display the correct QuickMenu.

Adding or Deleting Rows and Columns

To insert one or more rows or columns into your table, perform the following steps:

1. Move the cursor to the row or column next to which you want to add the new row or column.

2. Open the Table menu and select Insert. The Insert Columns/Rows dialog box appears (see figure 22.3).

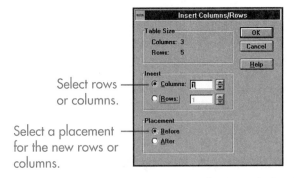

Select rows or columns.

Select a placement for the new rows or columns.

Figure 22.3   Insert rows or columns with this dialog box.

3. Select Rows or Columns, then enter the number of rows or columns you want to insert in the text box next to your selection.

4. Select Before or After to specify where you want the rows or columns inserted.

5. Click OK. WordPerfect inserts your rows or columns.

To delete rows or columns, highlight the rows or columns you want to delete and select Table Delete. In the Delete dialog box, indicate the appropriate number of rows or columns, and then click OK. Your rows or columns are removed.

Adjusting the Column Width

When you create a table, WordPerfect makes the table as wide as possible and makes the columns all the same width. You can adjust the column width by performing the following steps:

1. Position your mouse pointer between two columns so the pointer turns into a horizontal double-headed arrow bisected by a vertical line.

2. Click and drag the column to the desired width, and release the mouse button.

Other Formatting Options

You can format the table using any of the techniques you learned when formatting text. For example, you can select a cell and click on the Bold button on the Toolbar to make the cell's contents bold. Change the font or font size of a cell's contents with the Power Bar. The next few sections explain some special options that make formatting a table easier.

Formatting Numbers

Format the numbers in a cell by selecting the cells you want to format and selecting Table Number Type, or click on the Number Type button on the Tables Toolbar. Choose a type from the dialog box that appears, then click OK.

How Do I Select a Cell? To select cells, move the cursor to the first cell and drag to select the cells you want. To select the entire table, move the cursor to any edge (a selection arrow appears) and triple-click the mouse button.

Adding Lines and Fills

Format the cells themselves with the Lines Fill command on the Table menu. Select the cells you want to format, select the command or click on the Lines/Fill button on the Tables Toolbar, and select the Line Style and Fill Options you want. You can format any of the four sides of a cell, and the inside or outside edges of a selection. To format the entire table, click on the Table option at the top of the dialog box.

Joining and Splitting Cells

You can join cells together to form one big cell (see the title cell in the table shown in Figure 22.1). Select the cells to join, then select Table Join Cell. To split a cell into smaller cells, select it and choose Table Split Cell. Enter the number of rows or columns into which you want your cell split, and click OK.

Using the Table Expert

Automatically format the table with the Table Expert. Select the Table Expert command, or click on the Table Expert button on the Tables Toolbar. Select from the list of Available Styles. The sample changes to reflect your choice. Click on Apply to apply the style to your table.

In this lesson, you learned how to create a table and the basics of how to format the table. In the next lesson, you'll learn how to search for and replace text within a document.

Lesson

Finding and Replacing Text

In this lesson, you'll learn how to find a word or phrase in a document and (if you want) replace that word or phrase with a different word or phrase.

Searching for a Text String

WordPerfect can find any text or formatting code in a document. If you want to replace the word, phrase, or formatting code with something else once you find it, refer to the "Replacing Text or Codes" section later in this lesson. To simply search for text, perform the following steps:

1. Move the cursor where you want the search to start. You can search forward or backward from this position. (To start from the beginning of the document, press Ctrl+Home.)

2. Open the Edit menu and select Find and Replace, or press F2. The Find and Replace Text dialog box appears, as shown in Figure 23.1.

3. Type the text for which you want WordPerfect to search.

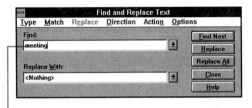

Type the text to search for.

Figure 23.1 Use the Find and Replace Text dialog box to specify the text you want to find.

4. You can choose one or more of the following options:

- Open the Type menu and select Word Forms to have WordPerfect search for all forms of a word. For example, if you type the word **have** in the text box and select Word Forms, WordPerfect will find **have**, **has**, and **had**.

- Open the Match menu and select special criteria that you want matched, such as the same case (upper or lower), the entire word, or a particular font.

- Open the Direction menu and specify in which direction (forward or backward) you want to search. (The default is to search from the cursor to the end of the document.)

- Open the Action menu and specify where you want the cursor to end up when WordPerfect finds the text. The default is to select the found text, but you can also position the cursor before or after the text, or extend the selection.

- Open the Options menu and specify where to search, such as from the top to the bottom, from the present point back to the present point again, and so on. You can also indicate whether or not to search headers and footers.

5. Click on Find Next to begin the search. WordPerfect hunts down the first occurrence of the specified word or phrase and moves to it.

6. Repeat step 5 to find more occurrences of the word or phrase.

7. Click on Close to stop searching.

Searching for Formatting Codes

In the previous steps, you entered a text string to have WordPerfect search for a specific word or phrase. It is often useful to search for hidden codes as well. For example, if you want to find all the bold text in a document, you can have WordPerfect search for the Bold On code.

Turn on Reveal Codes   When searching for formatting codes, it's a good idea to have the codes displayed. Press Alt+F3, or open the View menu and select Reveal Codes.

To search for a code, perform the following steps:

1. Move the cursor to the place where you want to start the search.

2. Open the Edit menu and select Find and Replace, or press F2. The Find and Replace Text dialog box appears.

3. Open the Match menu and select Codes. The Codes dialog box appears (see figure 23.2).

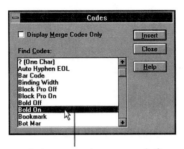

Select a code to search for.

Figure 23.2   The Codes dialog box.

4. Select the code you want to search for from the list, and click on Insert.

5. Repeat step 4 to insert additional codes for which to search. All codes must exist together in the document to be considered a match. For example, if you insert **[Bold On]** and **[Italc On]**, then a word must be *both* bold and italic to match.

6. When you're done, click on Close. You return to the Find and Replace Text dialog box. Click on Find Next to begin the search.

7. Click on Find Next to search for other occurrences of the code. To stop the search, click on Close.

> **Don't Type the Code!**   Although it looks like you could just type a code in the Find and Replace Text dialog box, if you type the code, WordPerfect searches for it as text, not as a formatting code. Therefore, you must select Codes from the Match menu and choose a code that way.

Get Specific If you need to search for a specific code, such as Center Justification (as opposed to simply Justification), open the Type menu in step 3 and select Specific Codes. Select the code you want from the list and click OK. Select the specifics you need, and click on Find Next to start the search.

Replacing Text or Codes

The Find and Replace feature allows you to replace the found word, phrase, or code with another word, phrase, or code. To replace text and/or codes, perform the following steps:

1. Move the cursor to the place where you want the find and replace operation to start. WordPerfect searches and replaces from the cursor position forward or back.

2. Open the Edit menu and select Find and Replace, or press F2. The Find and Replace Text dialog box appears, as shown in Figure 23.3.

Type the text to search for.

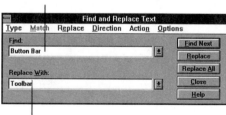

Type the text to replace the found text.

Figure 23.3 The Find and Replace Text dialog box.

3. In the Find text box, type the text you want to replace. Or open the Match menu and select Codes, and choose a code as you did earlier in this lesson.

Just the Specifics   You can find and replace a specific code (such as Font:Arial) by selecting NoType Specific Codes. In step 4, just enter the codes you want to replace the codes you find.

4. Type the text you want to substitute for the found text in the Replace With text box. (Again, you can use codes instead by selecting Match Codes.)

5. Select any of the other replacement options to control the search and replace operation. (Some of these options do not apply if you're searching and replacing hidden codes instead of text.)

   • Open the Type menu and select Word Forms to have WordPerfect search for all forms of a word. For example, if you type the word **have** in the text box and select Word Forms, WordPerfect will find **have**, **has**, and **had**.

   • Open the Replace menu and select special criteria that you want matched, such as the same case (upper or lower), the entire word, or a particular font.

   • Open the Direction menu and specify in which direction (forward or backward) you want to search. (The default is to search from the cursor to the end of the document.)

   • Open the Action menu and specify where you want the cursor to end up when the text is found. The default is to select the found text, but you can also position the cursor before or after the text, or extend the selection.

- Open the Options menu and specify where to search, such as from the top to the bottom, from the present point back to the present point again, and so on. You can also indicate whether or not to search headers and footers.

6. **(Optional)** To replace the found code with nothing, click on Replace with Nothing.

7. Click the Replace button to replace the first instance, or the Replace All button to replace every instance at once. If WordPerfect cannot find the text or code you want to replace, you'll get a message to that effect.

8. Select Close when you finish to close the dialog box.

In this lesson, you learned how to have WordPerfect find and optionally replace specific text and codes. In the next lesson, you learn how to use WordPerfect's writing tools to further polish your documents.

Lesson

Using WordPerfect's Writing Tools

In this lesson, you'll learn how to use WordPerfect's writing tools: Spell Checker, Grammatik, and Thesaurus.

Checking Your Spelling

WordPerfect has a program that can check your document for spelling errors and provide a list of possible corrections. You can check the spelling of a single word or page, or the entire document. To run Spell Checker, perform the following steps:

1. **(Optional)** To spell check part of a document only, select the text whose spelling you want to check. (To spell check the entire document, the cursor can be anywhere.)

2. Click on the Spell Check button on the Toolbar, or select Tools/Spell Check. The Spell Checker dialog box appears, and Spell Checker begins checking your document. When Spell Checker finds a word that is not in its dictionary, it displays the word along with some alternatives from which to choose, as shown in Figure 24.1.

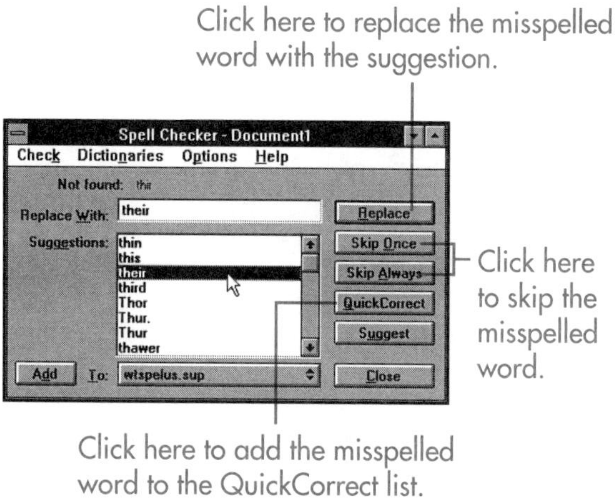

Click here to replace the misspelled
word with the suggestion.

Click here
to skip the
misspelled
word.

Click here to add the misspelled
word to the QuickCorrect list.

Figure 24.1   When Spell Checker finds a word it doesn't
recognize, it lists some alternatives for you.

3. Take one of the following actions to respond to
Spell Checker:

   • Highlight the correct spelling in the Sugges-
     tions list and click on Replace.

   • Prod Spell Checker for more suggestions by
     typing an alternate spelling for the word in
     the Replace With box, and clicking on the
     Suggest button.

   • If Spell Checker can't provide the correct
     spelling suggestion, type the correction
     yourself in the Replace With text box, and
     click on Replace.

   • If this is a common misspelling for you, add it
     to the QuickCorrect feature, which will
     automatically correct it as you type your
     document (See Lesson 4). Type the correc-
     tion in the Replace With text box, and click
     on QuickCorrect. WordPerfect corrects the

word in the document, and adds the word to the QuickCorrect list.

- Choose Skip Once to skip this occurrence of the word.

- Choose Skip Always to skip all occurrences of the word.

- Choose Add to add the word to the dictionary.

4. (Optional) To quit Spell Checker at any time, select Close.

5. When the spell check is complete, click on Yes to return to your document.

Proofread Your Document   WordPerfect questions only those words that do not match a word in Spell Checker's dictionary. For example, if you type "your" when you mean "you're," Spell Check skips over the error.

Checking Your Grammar

WordPerfect contains a built-in grammar checker (Grammatik) that can check your document for grammatical problems, such as overuse of the passive voice, misplaced commas, and subject-verb disagreement. Grammatik also checks the spelling of your document. To check a document, perform the following steps:

1. Click on the Grammatik button on the Toolbar or select Tools/Grammatik. Grammatik starts to check the grammar and spelling of the current document and stops on the first problem it finds, as shown in Figure 24.2.

Select a suggestion and click on Replace.

Grammatik [English-U.S.] - Document1

Check Preferences View Dictionaries Help

Replacements:	isn't aren't am not		Replace
New Sentence:	It isn't got that swing if you ain't got that thing.		Skip Once
			Skip Always
Special-Case Spelling:	Avoid this nonstandard expression in writing.		Add
			Undo
Checking Style:	Quick Check	Rule	Close

Click here to skip the problem.

Figure 24.2 Grammatik finds a wide variety of grammar problems and offers to correct them for you.

2. If Grammatik stops on a problem, do one of the following:

- Select Replace to have Grammatik correct the problem.

- Select Skip Once to skip this problem.

- Select Skip Always to skip all occurrences of this problem.

- Select Undo to undo a correction.

- Click in the document and type a correction, then click on Resume.

3. To quit Grammatik any time during the grammar check, select Close.

4. When the grammar check is complete, click on Yes to return to your document.

More About Grammatik Grammatik is a powerful and complex grammar checking program. For example, try changing the Checking Style to find a grammatical style that fits the way you write.

Choosing the Best Word with the Thesaurus

WordPerfect has a thesaurus that can help you find a synonym (a word that has a similar meaning) for one of the words in your document. To view a list of synonyms for a word, perform the following steps:

1. Move the cursor inside the word whose synonyms you want to view.

2. Select Tools/Thesaurus or press Alt+F1. The Thesaurus dialog box appears (see Figure 24.3).

A list of synonyms for this word appears in the last column.

The original word

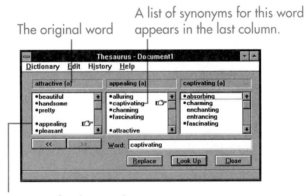

A list of synonyms for this word appears in the middle column.

Figure 24.3 The Thesaurus provides a list of synonyms for the selected word.

3. To replace the highlighted word with one of the words in the list, highlight the desired word in the list and select Replace.

4. Click on Close to return to your document.

Expanding the List of Synonyms

Notice that the thesaurus divides into three columns and that some of the words in the first column are preceded by a dot. If you select a word that is preceded by a dot, a list of synonyms for that word appears in the next column. To view a list of synonyms for a word in the list, perform the following steps:

1. Double-click on the word whose synonyms you want to view (it must be preceded by a dot).

2. Repeat step 1 in the new column to view another list of synonyms.

> **Shifting Columns**   If you choose to view more than two additional columns, the original column remains on-screen, but the other columns start to move off the screen to the left. To bring those columns into view, click on the left arrow button at the bottom of the Thesaurus dialog box until the desired column appears. You can then use the right arrow button to view columns that scroll off the right side of the screen.

Looking Up a Word

In addition to viewing synonyms for a word that's already in the document, you can type a word and have WordPerfect find synonyms for that word. To look up a word, perform the following steps:

1. Type a word you want to look up in the Word text box.

2. Click on Look Up .

Viewing a List of Words You Have Looked Up   The History menu displays a list of all the words you have looked up. To move to the column of synonyms for a word quickly, open the History menu and select the word from the list.

In this lesson, you learned how to use WordPerfect's writing tools to help you polish your documents. In the next lesson, you will learn how to add graphic objects to a document.

Lesson 25

Adding Graphic Objects to a Document

In this lesson, you'll learn how to add WordPerfect clip art to your document. You'll also learn how to add graphic lines and text boxes.

Adding WordPerfect Clip Art to Your Document

WordPerfect comes with several clip art images that you can add to your documents to spruce them up. For example, you can add a clip art image to a letter to create a customized letterhead or accent your newsletters with pictures. To insert a clip art image into your document, perform the following steps:

1. Open the Graphics menu. Make sure the Drag to Create option is turned on. (If the option is on, a checkmark appears next to it. If it isn't on, click on it.)

2. Open the Graphics menu again and select Image.

3. Click to establish the left-hand corner of the image, and drag downward and to the right (see Figure 25.1). You will select the image in step 4 to place in the box that you draw here.

Click to establish the left corner.

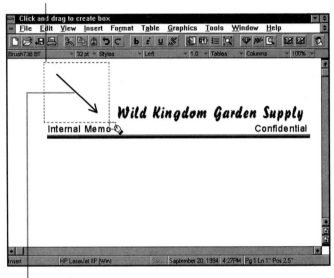

Drag downward and to the right.

Figure 25.1   Draw the box into which you will place the image.

4. The Insert Image dialog box, shown in Figure 25.2, appears. Select the image you want from the Filename list (change the directory on the Directories list if needed) and click OK.

WordPerfect creates a graphics box in your document and inserts the graphic. (The clip art files have the extension .WPG, which stands for WordPerfect Graphic.)

Can I Use Other Clip Art?   If you want to insert a graphic other than the WordPerfect clip art (with .WPG extensions), choose the type you want to insert (such as .BMP files) from the List Files of Type drop-down list.

Select an image to insert.

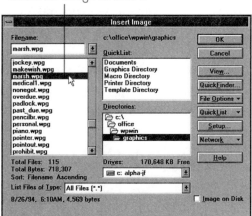

Figure 25.2   Select an image to insert with this dialog box.

Quick Viewing   Before you commit to an image, it may be nice to see what it looks like. Click on the View button to open a viewing window, and click on various graphics file names until you see one you like.

5. When you import a graphic into WordPerfect, the Graphics Box feature bar appears at the top of the document editing window to help you in editing the figure (covered later in this lesson). If you don't want to do anything right now to change the graphic, click on the Close button on the Graphics Box feature bar to return to your document.

Quick Image   You can insert an image quickly by clicking on the Image button on the Toolbar. WordPerfect places the image you select into a standard sized box that you can later resize.

By the way, clip art images are not the only way to add color and interest to a document; see Lesson 27 for tips on using WordPerfect Draw to create your own art.

Moving, Resizing, or Deleting an Object

To move, resize, or delete an object, select it first by clicking on it. Handles (small black boxes) appear around the perimeter of the object.

- To change the size of the object, click on one of the handles and drag it until the dotted outline of the object is the desired size and dimensions. (Drag a side handle to change one dimension at a time; drag a corner handle to change two dimensions.)

- To move the object, move the mouse pointer anywhere over the object. The mouse pointer changes to a four-sided arrow. Drag the object where you want it, then release the mouse button.

- To delete the object, press Delete.

Changing an Object's Appearance

You can change an object's appearance with the Graphics Box feature bar. The feature bar offers far too many features to discuss here, but Table 25.1 provides a quick summary of your options:

Displaying the Feature Bar   If the feature bar is no longer displayed, click on the object to select it. Click on the object with the right mouse button, and select Feature Bar from the QuickMenu.

Table 25.1 Graphic Box feature bar buttons.

Button	Purpose
Caption	Assigns a caption to the graphics box.
Content	Lets you change and center the image in the box.
Position	Controls the position of the graphics box in relation to the text of the document.
Size	Allows you to set a precise size for the graphics box.
Border/Fill	Controls the width, color, and pattern of the graphics box's border and interior. See Lesson 20 for tips on using the Border/Fill dialog box.
Wrap	Controls how text wraps around the box and its object.
Style	Changes the graphics box type.
Tools	Opens the Image Tools, a "box" of editing tools you can use to change the object.
Next	Moves to the next graphics box in the document, if there is more than one.
Previous	Moves to the previous graphics box in the document, if there is more than one.
Close	Returns you to your document.

Adding Graphics Lines to Your Document

In addition to clip art, you can accent your documents by adding vertical (up and down) or horizontal (left to right) lines to your document. To add a line to your document, perform the following steps:

1. Move the cursor to where you want the line to appear.

2. For a horizontal line, select Horizontal Line from the Graphics menu, or press Ctrl+F11. For a vertical line, select Vertical Line, or press Ctrl+Shift+F11. A vertical or horizontal line appears, with a default length, style, and thickness.

Line Up! To change the appearance of a graphics line, click on the line to select it, then click the right mouse button. Select Edit Line. From this dialog box, you can change the line style, length, position, color, and thickness.

Adding a Text Box

A text box is a special type of graphics box that contains text. You can move a text box anywhere in your document (to create a sidebar for example). To create a text box:

1. If necessary, open the Graphics menu and select Drag to Create. A check mark appears next to the option, indicating that it is on.

2. Open the Graphics menu again and select Text Box, or click on the Text Box button on the Toolbar. (The Text Box button is only visible when you move the Toolbar into the work area.)

3. Click to establish the left-hand corner of the image, and drag downward and to the right.

4. Type your text into the box. You can change the font style and font size with the Power Bar.

5. When you create a text box, the Graphics Box feature bar appears at the top of the document editing window to help you in changing how the text box looks (see earlier in this lesson). If you don't want to do anything right now to change the text box, click on the Close button on the Graphics Box feature bar to return to the document.

> **Fast Text**   You can also create a text box without using the Drag to Create feature. With the Drag to Create option off, select Graphics Text Box. A text box of a default size and border appears at the cursor.

To create special text effects, such as rotated or twisted text, use TextArt. See Lesson 26 for more information.

In this lesson, you learned how to add clip art, graphics lines, and text boxes to your document. In the next lesson, you'll learn how to use TextArt.

Lesson

Rotating, Stretching, and Contorting Text

In this lesson, you'll learn how to twist and rotate text with TextArt.

Starting TextArt

WordPerfect 6.1 for Windows comes with a nice text manipulation program called TextArt. With it, you can rotate, stretch, and contort text to create interesting effects for your documents. To start TextArt:

- Click on the TextArt button on the Toolbar.

  OR

- Open the Graphics menu and select TextArt.

    A graphics box appears. Your TextArt will go there. The TextArt dialog box also appears, as shown in Figure 26.1. See the next section for steps in using TextArt to create the effect you want.

Using TextArt

To create your TextArt, follow these steps:

1. Type your text into the text box. You can use up to three lines of text. To insert special characters such as ½ or ¼, click on the Character select button.

Rotate
Justification
Text outline color
Text outline width
Shadow color
Shadow position
Text pattern
Character select

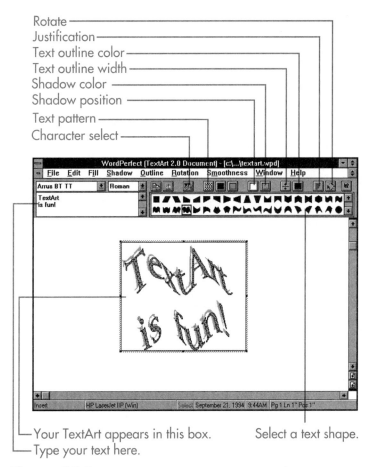

Your TextArt appears in this box.   Select a text shape.
Type your text here.

Figure 26.1   TextArt allows you to create fun text effects.

2. (Optional) Choose a different font or attribute.

3. Select a text shape by clicking on it.

4. (Optional) Change text fill by clicking on the Text pattern button, and/or changing the foreground or background colors.

5. (Optional) Add a shadow and/or change the shadow color.

6. **(Optional)** Change the color or width of the text outline.

7. **(Optional)** Change the justification and/or rotate the TextArt within the graphics box.

8. When you finish, simply click inside the document.

You can resize, move, and delete your TextArt, and even change the characteristics of the graphics box that surrounds it. For example, you can remove the border of the graphics box. To make changes to the TextArt itself, double-click on it.

In this lesson, you learned how to create TextArt. In the next lesson, you'll learn how to create art with WordPerfect Draw.

Lesson 27

Working with WordPerfect Draw

In this lesson, you'll learn how to create art to enhance your documents with WordPerfect Draw.

Starting WordPerfect Draw

With WordPerfect Draw, you can create artwork such as a company logo, small clip art for a newsletter, or charts for a report. To start WordPerfect Draw:

- Open the Graphics menu and select Draw to create a new drawing.

   OR

- Click on the Draw or Chart buttons on the Toolbar. (The Draw and Chart buttons are only visible when you move the Toolbar into the work area.)

   OR

- Double-click on an existing drawing to edit it.

Using the Tool Palette

When you start WordPerfect Draw, it opens a graphics box in which you will create your drawing. The Tool Palette appears on the left; you select drawing tools from it to create your artwork. A special Toolbar appears at the top of the window from which you can select commands to save your drawing, display gridlines which help you align objects, and flip your artwork vertically or horizontally.

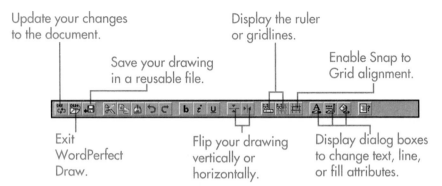

Update your changes
to the document.

Save your drawing
in a reusable file.

Display the ruler
or gridlines.

Enable Snap to
Grid alignment.

Exit
WordPerfect
Draw.

Flip your drawing
vertically or
horizontally.

Display dialog boxes
to change text, line,
or fill attributes.

Figure 27.1 The Drawing Toolbar.

Read the description of each tool on the Tool Palette in Table 27.1. Some buttons, such as the Text Object Tools button, open to display the actual tools from which you must chose. In those cases, only the current selection appears on the Tool Palette.

Table 27.1 The Tool Palette.

Button	Purpose
	Selects an object in the drawing.
	Inserts a clip art file into the drawing.
	Creates a chart.
	Creates a text box in which the text appears on a long line.
	Creates a text box in which text wraps.
	Creates a rectangle.
	Creates a rectangle with rounded corners.
	Creates a multisided object (polygon).
	Creates an oval.

Button	Purpose
♥	Creates an object with curves.
◉	Creates a perfect circle.
/	Creates a straight line.
⌐	Creates a curved line.
C	Creates part of an ellipsis.
✎	Allows you to draw freehand.
⋯	Sets the line width.
▦	Sets the fill pattern.
▰	Sets the line color.
▣	Sets the fill colors.

Drawing Objects

To select a tool, click on it. To create an object with a tool, follow the appropriate steps.

Before You Start Before you draw your object, set the line style, line width, fill colors, and pattern. You can abort drawing an object by pressing Esc. If you want to delete a completed object, click on it and press Delete.

True Artist If you need to, press both mouse buttons while drawing an object to reposition it within the drawing area. While drawing straight-edged objects such as a polygon, press and hold the Shift key to create perfect 90 or 45 degree angles.

Creating a Closed Object (Rectangle or Circle)

1. Click on the Closed Object Tools button and select a tool.

2. Click in the drawing area to establish the upper left-hand corner of the object.

3. Hold down the mouse button, and drag to the lower right-hand corner of the object. A faint outline of the object follows your mouse pointer.

4. Release the mouse button and the completed object appears.

Creating a Multisided Object (Polygon or Closed Curve)

1. Click on the Closed Object Tools or Line Object button and select a tool, such as Polygon, Closed Curve, or Curved Line.

2. Click in the drawing area to establish the upper left-hand corner of the object.

3. Click again to establish the next point. A line connects the two points.

4. Repeat step 3 to add additional sides to a polygon or change the direction of the curve for a closed curve or curved line.

5. Double-click the mouse button to establish the last point and to complete the object.

Creating a Line

1. Click on the Line Object Tools button and select the Line tool.

2. Click in the drawing area to establish the beginning of the line.

3. **(Optional)** Click again to establish the next point. A line connects the two points. Repeat to add additional lines to create a zigzag.

4. Double-click the mouse button to establish the last point and to complete the line.

Drawing Freehand

1. Click on the Line Objects Tools button and select the Freehand tool.

2. Click in the drawing area to establish the beginning of your object.

3. Drag the mouse pointer around the drawing area like you would a pencil.

4. To complete your object, release the mouse button.

Adding Text

1. Click on the Text Object Tools button and select a tool.

2. **(Optional)** If you selected the Text Area tool, drag to create the text box.

3. **(Optional)** Change the font style or font size with the Power Bar.

4. Type your text. When you finish, click inside the drawing or select another tool.

Adding a Clip Art Image

1. Click on the QuickArt tool.

2. Drag to create a box in which to place the clip art. The Insert Image dialog box appears.

3. Select an image to insert, and click OK.

Manipulating Objects

Several objects can comprise a single drawing, as shown in Figure 27.2. Before you can make changes to any of these objects, you must select them.

Curved line objects   Closed curve object

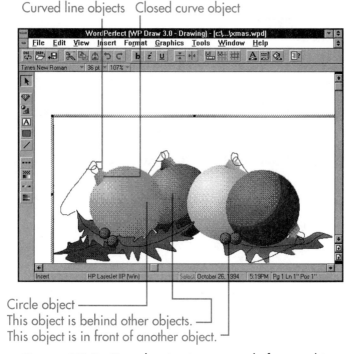

Circle object
This object is behind other objects.
This object is in front of another object.

Figure 27.2 Your drawing is composed of many objects.

- Select an object by clicking on the Select tool and clicking on the object.

- You can select several objects at once by pressing Shift as you click on them.

- To select all the objects in a drawing, open the Edit menu, choose Select, and choose All.

You can even permanently group some objects together so that they move and act as a single unit. Select the objects you want to group, open the Graphics menu, and select Group. You can later ungroup these objects by selecting Graphics/Separate.

You can move, resize, or delete these objects using the same steps that you learned in Lesson 25. To change the fill color, fill pattern, or outline of an object, select it and make your changes.

Fine Points   You can correct the shape of an object by manipulating the invisible points on which it is based. To display these invisible points, double-click on the object (such as a polygon, line rectangle, or ellipse), and drag one of the points to a new location. WordPerfect Draw automatically redraws the object, based on the new points.

WordPerfect Draw arranges the objects in the drawing area in layers, one on top of the other in places where their respective outlines overlap. You can reposition objects in the stack (in other words, move one object in front of another or vice-versa) by following these steps:

1. Select the object whose position in the stack you want to change.

2. Open the Graphics menu and select Order.

3. Select either Front or Back.

In this lesson, you learned how to create art with WordPerfect Draw. This is the last lesson in the book; you are now familiar with all of WordPerfect's basic features. Feel free to try some of the more advanced features on your own. Good luck, and good writing!

Index